www.EffortlessMath.com

... So Much More Online!

✓ FREE Math lessons

✓ More Math learning books!

✓ Mathematics Worksheets

✓ Online Math Tutors

Need a PDF version of this book?

Please visit www.EffortlessMath.com

HSPT Math Study Guide 2021- 2022

Step-By-Step Guide to Preparing for the HSPT Math Test

By

Reza Nazari

All inquiries should be addressed to:
info@effortlessMath.com
www.EffortlessMath.com

ISBN: 978-1-63719-035-7

Published by: **Effortless Math Education Inc.**

For Online Math Practice Visit www.EffortlessMath.com

Welcome to
HSPT Math Prep
2021

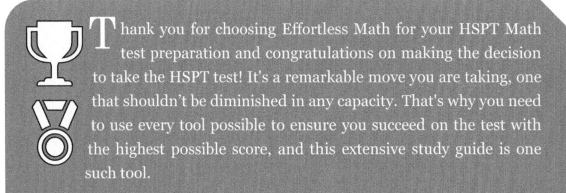

Thank you for choosing Effortless Math for your HSPT Math test preparation and congratulations on making the decision to take the HSPT test! It's a remarkable move you are taking, one that shouldn't be diminished in any capacity. That's why you need to use every tool possible to ensure you succeed on the test with the highest possible score, and this extensive study guide is one such tool.

If math has never been a strong subject for you, **don't worry**! This book will help you prepare for (and even ACE) the HSPT test's math section. As test day draws nearer, effective preparation becomes increasingly more important. Thankfully, you have this comprehensive study guide to help you get ready for the test. With this guide, you can feel confident that you will be more than ready for the HSPT Math test when the time comes.

First and foremost, it is important to note that this book is a study guide and not a textbook. It is best read from cover to cover. Every lesson of this "self-guided math book" was carefully developed to ensure that you are making the most effective use of your time while preparing for the test. This up-to-date guide reflects the 2021 test guidelines and will put you on the right track to hone your math skills, overcome exam anxiety, and boost your confidence, so that you can have your best to succeed on the HSPT Math test.

This study guide will:

☑ Explain the format of the HSPT Math test.

☑ Describe specific test-taking strategies that you can use on the test.

☑ Provide HSPT Math test-taking tips.

☑ Review all HSPT Math concepts and topics you will be tested on.

☑ Help you identify the areas in which you need to concentrate your study time.

☑ Offer exercises that help you develop the basic math skills you will learn in each section.

☑ Give **2 realistic and full-length practice tests** (featuring new question types) with detailed answers to help you measure your exam readiness and build confidence.

This resource contains everything you will ever need to succeed on the HSPT Math test. You'll get in-depth instructions on every math topic as well as tips and techniques on how to answer each question type. You'll also get plenty of practice questions to boost your test-taking confidence.

In addition, in the following pages you'll find:

➢ **How to Use This Book Effectively** – This section provides you with step-by-step instructions on how to get the most out of this comprehensive study guide.

➢ **How to study for the HSPT Math Test** – A six-step study program has been developed to help you make the best use of this book and prepare for your HSPT Math test. Here you'll find tips and strategies to guide your study program and help you understand HSPT Math and how to ace the test.

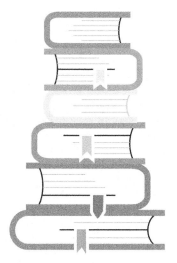

➢ **HSPT Math Review** – Learn everything you need to know about the HSPT Math test.

➢ **HSPT Math Test-Taking Strategies** – Learn how to effectively put these recommended test-taking techniques into use for improving your HSPT Math score.

➢ **Test Day Tips** – Review these tips to make sure you will do your best when the big day comes.

Effortless Math's HSPT Online Center

Effortless Math Online HSPT Center offers a complete study program, including the following:

✓ Step-by-step instructions on how to prepare for the HSPT Math test

✓ Numerous HSPT Math worksheets to help you measure your math skills

✓ Complete list of HSPT Math formulas

✓ Video lessons for all HSPT Math topics

✓ Full-length HSPT Math practice tests

✓ And much more...

No Registration Required.

Visit effortlessmath.com/HSPT to find your online HSPT Math resources.

How to Use This Book Effectively

Look no further when you need a study guide to improve your math skills to succeed on the math portion of the HSPT test. Each chapter of this comprehensive guide to the HSPT Math will provide you with the knowledge, tools, and understanding needed for every topic covered on the test.

It's imperative that you understand each topic before moving onto another one, as that's the way to guarantee your success. Each topic provides you with examples and a step-by-step guide of every concept to better understand the content that will be on the test. To get the best possible results from this book:

➢ **Begin studying long before your test date**. This provides you ample time to learn the different math concepts. The earlier you begin studying for the test, the sharper your skills will be. Do not procrastinate! Provide yourself with plenty of time to learn the concepts and feel comfortable that you understand them when your test date arrives.

➢ **Practice consistently**. Study HSPT Math concepts at least 20 to 30 minutes a day. Remember, slow and steady wins the race, which can be applied to preparing for the HSPT Math test. Instead of cramming to tackle everything at once, be patient and learn the math topics in short bursts.

➢ Whenever you get a math problem wrong, **mark it off, and review it later** to make sure you understand the concept.

➢ Start each session by **looking over the previous material.**

➢ Once you've reviewed the book's lessons, **take the practice test at the back of the book** to gauge your level of readiness. Then, review your results. Read detailed answers and solutions for each question you missed.

➢ **Take another practice test** to get an idea of how ready you are to take the actual exam. Taking the practice tests will give you the confidence you need on test day. Simulate the HSPT testing environment by sitting in a quiet room free from distraction. Make sure to clock yourself with a timer.

How to Study for the HSPT Math Test

Studying for the HSPT Math test can be a really daunting and boring task. What's the best way to go about it? Is there a certain study method that works better than others? Well, studying for the HSPT Math can be done effectively. The following six-step program has been designed to make preparing for the HSPT Math test more efficient and less overwhelming.

Step **1** - Create a study plan
Step **2** - Choose your study resources
Step **3** - Review, Learn, Practice
Step **4** - Learn and practice test-taking strategies
Step **5** - Learn the HSPT Test format and take practice tests
Step **6** - Analyze your performance

STEP **1**: Create a Study Plan

It's always easier to get things done when you have a plan. Creating a study plan for the HSPT Math test can help you to stay on track with your studies. It's important to sit down and prepare a study plan with what works with your life, work, and any other obligations you may have. Devote enough time each day to studying. It's also a great idea to break down each section of the exam into blocks and study one concept at a time.

It's important to understand that there is no "right" way to create a study plan. Your study plan will be personalized based on your specific needs and learning style. Follow these guidelines to create an effective study plan for your HSPT Math test:

★ **Analyze your learning style and study habits** – Everyone has a different learning style. It is essential to embrace your individuality and the unique way you learn. Think about what works and what doesn't work for you. Do you prefer HSPT Math prep books or a combination of textbooks and video lessons? Does it work better for you if you study every night for thirty minutes or is it more effective to study in the morning before going to work?

★ **Evaluate your schedule** – Review your current schedule and find out how much time you can consistently devote to HSPT Math study.

★ **Develop a schedule** – Now it's time to add your study schedule to your calendar like any other obligation. Schedule time for study, practice, and review. Plan out which topic you will study on which day to ensure that you're devoting enough time to each concept. Develop a study plan that is mindful, realistic, and flexible.

★ **Stick to your schedule** – A study plan is only effective when it is followed consistently. You should try to develop a study plan that you can follow for the length of your study program.

★ **Evaluate your study plan and adjust as needed** – Sometimes you need to adjust your plan when you have new commitments. Check in with yourself regularly to make sure that you're not falling behind in your study plan. Remember, the most important thing is sticking to your plan. Your study plan is all about helping you be more productive. If you find that your study plan is not as effective as you want, don't get discouraged. It's okay to make changes as you figure out what works best for you.

STEP 2: Choose Your Study Resources

There are numerous textbooks and online resources available for the HSPT Math test, and it may not be clear where to begin. Don't worry! This study guide provides everything you need to fully prepare for your HSPT Math test. In addition to the book content, you can also use Effortless Math's online resources. (video lessons, worksheets, formulas, etc.) On each page, there is a link (and a QR code) to an online webpage

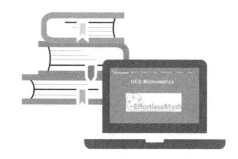

which provides a comprehensive review of the topic, step-by-step instruction, video tutorial, and numerous examples and exercises to help you fully understand the concept.

You can also visit EffortlessMath.com/HSPT to find your online HSPT Math resources.

STEP 3: Review, Learn, Practice

This HSPT Math study guide breaks down each subject into specific skills or content areas. For instance, the percent concept is separated into different topics–percent calculation, percent increase and decrease, percent problems, etc. Use this study guide and Effortless Math online HSPT center to help you go over all key math concepts and topics on the HSPT Math test.

As you read each topic, take notes or highlight the concepts you would like to go over again in the future. If you're unfamiliar with a topic or something is difficult for you, use the link (or the QR code) at the bottom of the page to find the webpage that provides more instruction about that topic. For each math topic, plenty of instructions, step-by-step guides, and examples are provided to ensure you get a good grasp of the material.

Quickly review the topics you do understand to get a brush-up of the material. Be sure to do the practice questions provided at the end of every chapter to measure your understanding of the concepts.

STEP 4: Learn and Practice Test-taking Strategies

In the following sections, you will find important test-taking strategies and tips that can help you earn extra points. You'll learn how to think strategically and when to guess if you don't know the answer to a question. Using HSPT Math test-taking strategies and tips can help you raise your score and do well on the test. Apply test taking strategies on the practice tests to help you boost your confidence.

STEP 5: Learn the HSPT Test Format and Take Practice Tests

The HSPT *Test Review* section provides information about the structure of the HSPT test. Read this section to learn more about the HSPT test structure, different test sections, the number of questions in each section, and the section time limits. When you have a prior understanding of the test format and different types of HSPT Math questions, you'll feel more confident when you take the actual exam.

Once you have read through the instructions and lessons and feel like you are ready to go – take advantage of both of the full-length HSPT Math practice tests available in this study guide. Use the practice tests to sharpen your skills and build confidence.

The HSPT Math practice tests offered at the end of the book are formatted similarly to the actual HSPT Math test. When you take each practice test, try to simulate actual testing conditions. To take the practice tests, sit in a quiet space, time yourself, and work through as many of the questions as time allows. The practice tests are followed by detailed answer explanations to help you find your weak areas, learn from your mistakes, and raise your HSPT Math score.

STEP 6: Analyze Your Performance

After taking the practice tests, look over the answer keys and explanations to learn which questions you answered correctly and which you did not. Never be discouraged if you make a few mistakes. See them as a learning opportunity. This will highlight your strengths and weaknesses.

You can use the results to determine if you need additional practice or if you are ready to take the actual HSPT Math test.

Looking for more?

Visit effortlessmath.com/HSPT to find hundreds of HSPT Math worksheets, video tutorials, practice tests, HSPT Math formulas, and much more.

Or scan this QR code.

No Registration Required.

HSPT Test Review

The High School Placement Test (HSPT), also known as STS-HSPT, formulated by the Scholastic Testing Service (STS) to determine acceptance in parochial high schools.

The HSPT test consists of five multiple-choice sections:

- ✓ **Verbal Skills:** 60 questions - 16 minutes
- ✓ **Quantitative Skills:** 52 questions - 30 minutes
- ✓ **Reading:** 62 questions - 25 minutes
- ✓ **Mathematics:** 64 questions - 45 minutes
- ✓ **Language:** 60 questions - 25 minutes

Keep in mind that the Quantitative Skills and the Mathematics sections are different parts. The Quantitative Skills section contains 52 questions providing number series, geometric comparisons, and number manipulation, whereas the Mathematics part measures students' math knowledge. The Math section of the test covers arithmetic, data analysis, geometry, and algebra.

Some schools allow students to use basic calculators when taking the HSPT test.

HSPT Math Test-Taking Strategies

Here are some test-taking strategies that you can use to maximize your performance and results on the HSPT Math test.

#1 : Use This Approach To Answer Every HSPT Math Question

- Review the question to identify keywords and important information.

- Translate the keywords into math operations so you can solve the problem.

- Review the answer choices. What are the differences between answer choices?

- Draw or label a diagram if needed.

- Try to find patterns.

- Find the right method to answer the question. Use straightforward math, plug in numbers, or test the answer choices (backsolving).

- Double-check your work.

#2 : Use Educated Guessing

This approach is applicable to the problems you understand to some degree but cannot solve using straightforward math. In such cases, try to filter out as many answer choices as possible before picking an answer. In cases where you don't have a clue about what a certain problem entails, don't waste any time trying to eliminate answer choices. Just choose one randomly before moving onto the next question.

As you can ascertain, direct solutions are the most optimal approach. Carefully read through the question, determine what the solution is using the math you have learned before, then coordinate the answer with one of the choices available to you. Are you stumped? Make your best guess, then move on.

Don't leave any fields empty! Even if you're unable to work out a problem, strive to answer it. Take a guess if you have to. You will not lose points by getting an answer wrong, though you may gain a point by getting it correct!

#3 : BALLPARK

A ballpark answer is a rough approximation. When we become overwhelmed by calculations and figures, we end up making silly mistakes. A decimal that is moved by one unit can change an answer from right to wrong, regardless of the number of steps that you went through to get it. That's where ballparking can play a big part.

If you think you know what the correct answer may be (even if it's just a ballpark answer), you'll usually have the ability to eliminate a couple of choices. While answer choices are usually based on the average student error and/or values that are closely tied, you will still be able to weed out choices that are way far afield. Try to find answers that aren't in the proverbial ballpark when you're looking for a wrong answer on a multiple-choice question. This is an optimal approach to eliminating answers to a problem.

#4 : BACKSOLVING

A majority of questions on the HSPT Math test will be in multiple-choice format. Many test-takers prefer multiple-choice questions, as at least the answer is right there. You'll typically have four answers to pick from. You simply need to figure out which one is correct. Usually, the best way to go about doing so is "backsolving."

As mentioned earlier, direct solutions are the most optimal approach to answering a question. Carefully read through a problem, calculate a solution, then correspond the answer with one of the choices displayed in front of you. If you can't calculate a solution, your next best approach involves "backsolving."

When backsolving a problem, contrast one of your answer options against the problem you are asked, then see which of them is most relevant. More often than not, answer choices are listed in ascending or descending order. In such cases, try out the choices B or C. If it's not correct, you can go either down or up from there.

#5 : PLUGGING IN NUMBERS

"Plugging in numbers" is a strategy that can be applied to a wide range of different math problems on the HSPT Math test. This approach is typically used to simplify a challenging question so that it is more understandable. By using the strategy carefully, you can find the answer without too much trouble.

The concept is fairly straightforward–replace unknown variables in a problem with certain values. When selecting a number, consider the following:

- Choose a number that's basic (just not too basic). Generally, you should avoid choosing 1 (or even 0). A decent choice is 2.

- Try not to choose a number that is displayed in the problem.

- Make sure you keep your numbers different if you need to choose at least two of them.

- More often than not, choosing numbers merely lets you filter out some of your answer choices. As such, don't just go with the first choice that gives you the right answer.

- If several answers seem correct, then you'll need to choose another value and try again. This time, though, you'll just need to check choices that haven't been eliminated yet.

- If your question contains fractions, then a potential right answer may involve either an LCD (least common denominator) or an LCD multiple.

- 100 is the number you should choose when you are dealing with problems involving percentages.

HSPT Math – Test Day Tips

After practicing and reviewing all the math concepts you've been taught, and taking some HSPT mathematics practice tests, you'll be prepared for test day. Consider the following tips to be extra-ready come test time.

Before Your Test

What to do the night before:

- **Relax!** One day before your test, study lightly or skip studying altogether. You shouldn't attempt to learn something new, either. There are plenty of reasons why studying the evening before a big test can work against you. Put it this way–a marathoner wouldn't go out for a sprint before the day of a big race. Mental marathoners–such as yourself–should not study for any more than one hour 24 hours before a HSPT test. That's because your brain requires some rest to be at its best. The night before your exam, spend some time with family or friends, or read a book.

- **Avoid bright screens** - You'll have to get some good shuteye the night before your test. Bright screens (such as the ones coming from your laptop, TV, or mobile device) should be avoided altogether. Staring at such a screen will keep your brain up, making it hard to drift asleep at a reasonable hour.

- **Make sure your dinner is healthy** - The meal that you have for dinner should be nutritious. Be sure to drink plenty of water as well. Load up on your complex carbohydrates, much like a marathon runner would do. Pasta, rice, and potatoes are ideal options here, as are vegetables and protein sources.

- **Get your bag ready for test day** - The night prior to your test, pack your bag with your stationery, admissions pass, ID, and any other gear that you need. Keep the bag right by your front door.

- **Make plans to reach the testing site** - Before going to sleep, ensure that you understand precisely how you will arrive at the site of the test. If parking is something you'll have to find first, plan for it. If you're dependent on public transit, then review the schedule. You should also make sure that the train/bus/subway/streetcar you use will be running. Find out about road closures

as well. If a parent or friend is accompanying you, ensure that they understand what steps they have to take as well.

The Day of the Test

- **Get up reasonably early, but not too early.**

- **Have breakfast** - Breakfast improves your concentration, memory, and mood. As such, make sure the breakfast that you eat in the morning is healthy. The last thing you want to be is distracted by a grumbling tummy. If it's not your own stomach making those noises, another test taker close to you might be instead. Prevent discomfort or embarrassment by consuming a healthy breakfast. Bring a snack with you if you think you'll need it.

- **Follow your daily routine** - Do you watch Good Morning America each morning while getting ready for the day? Don't break your usual habits on the day of the test. Likewise, if coffee isn't something you drink in the morning, then don't take up the habit hours before your test. Routine consistency lets you concentrate on the main objective–doing the best you can on your test.

- **Wear layers** - Dress yourself up in comfortable layers. You should be ready for any kind of internal temperature. If it gets too warm during the test, take a layer off.

- **Get there on time** - The last thing you want to do is get to the test site late. Rather, you should be there 45 minutes prior to the start of the test. Upon your arrival, try not to hang out with anybody who is nervous. Any anxious energy they exhibit shouldn't influence you.

- **Leave the books at home** - No books should be brought to the test site. If you start developing anxiety before the test, books could encourage you to do some last-minute studying, which will only hinder you. Keep the books far away–better yet, leave them at home.

- **Make your voice heard** - If something is off, speak to a proctor. If medical attention is needed or if you'll require anything, consult the proctor prior to the start of the test. Any doubts you have should be clarified. You should be entering the test site with a state of mind that is completely clear.

■ **Have faith in yourself** - When you feel confident, you will be able to perform at your best. When you are waiting for the test to begin, envision yourself receiving an outstanding result. Try to see yourself as someone who knows all the answers, no matter what the questions are. A lot of athletes tend to use this technique–particularly before a big competition. Your expectations will be reflected by your performance.

During your test

■ **Be calm and breathe deeply** - You need to relax before the test, and some deep breathing will go a long way to help you do that. Be confident and calm. You got this. Everybody feels a little stressed out just before an evaluation of any kind is set to begin. Learn some effective breathing exercises. Spend a minute meditating before the test starts. Filter out any negative thoughts you have. Exhibit confidence when having such thoughts.

■ **Concentrate on the test** - Refrain from comparing yourself to anyone else. You shouldn't be distracted by the people near you or random noise. Concentrate exclusively on the test. If you find yourself irritated by surrounding noises, earplugs can be used to block sounds off close to you. Don't forget–the test is going to last several hours if you're taking more than one subject of the test. Some of that time will be dedicated to brief sections. Concentrate on the specific section you are working on during a particular moment. Do not let your mind wander off to upcoming or previous sections.

■ **Skip challenging questions** - Optimize your time when taking the test. Lingering on a single question for too long will work against you. If you don't know what the answer is to a certain question, use your best guess, and mark the question so you can review it later on. There is no need to spend time attempting to solve something you aren't sure about. That time would be better served handling the questions you can actually answer well. You will not be penalized for getting the wrong answer on a test like this.

- **Try to answer each question individually** - Focus only on the question you are working on. Use one of the test-taking strategies to solve the problem. If you aren't able to come up with an answer, don't get frustrated. Simply skip that question, then move onto the next one.

- **Don't forget to breathe!** Whenever you notice your mind wandering, your stress levels boosting, or frustration brewing, take a thirty-second break. Shut your eyes, drop your pencil, breathe deeply, and let your shoulders relax. You will end up being more productive when you allow yourself to relax for a moment.

- **Review your answer.** If you still have time at the end of the test, don't waste it. Go back and check over your answers. It is worth going through the test from start to finish to ensure that you didn't make a sloppy mistake somewhere.

- **Optimize your breaks** - When break time comes, use the restroom, have a snack, and reactivate your energy for the subsequent section. Doing some stretches can help stimulate your blood flow.

After your test

- **Take it easy** - You will need to set some time aside to relax and decompress once the test has concluded. There is no need to stress yourself out about what you could've said, or what you may have done wrong. At this point, there's nothing you can do about it. Your energy and time would be better spent on something that will bring you happiness for the remainder of your day.

- **Redoing the test** - Did you pass the test? Congratulations! Your hard work paid off! Passing this test means that you are now as knowledgeable as somebody who has graduated high school.

  If you have failed your test, though, don't worry! The test can be retaken. In such cases, you will need to follow the retake policy established by your state. You also need to re-register to take the exam again.

Contents

√ - know
x - no
m - maybe
r - need to review

Contents

Check off

Contents

Topic	Simplifying Fractions
Notes	✓ Evenly divide both the top and bottom of the fraction by $2, 3, 5, 7, \ldots$ etc. ✓ Continue until you can't go any further.
Example	**Simplify $\frac{36}{48}$** To simplify $\frac{36}{48}$, find a number that both 36 and 48 are divisible by. Both are divisible by 12. Then: $\frac{36}{48} = \frac{36 \div 12}{48 \div 12} = \frac{3}{4}$

Your Turn!		
	1) $\frac{3}{15} = \frac{1}{5}$	2) $\frac{11}{55} = \frac{1}{5}$
	3) $\frac{12}{48} = \frac{1}{4}$	4) $\frac{11}{99} = \frac{1}{9}$
	5) $\frac{15}{75} = \frac{1}{5}$	6) $\frac{25}{100} = \frac{1}{4}$
	7) $\frac{16}{72} =$	8) $\frac{32}{96} =$
	9) $\frac{15}{65} =$	10) $\frac{48}{92} =$

Find more at

bit.ly/3nOGNko

Topic	Simplifying Fractions – Answers
Notes	✓ Evenly divide both the top and bottom of the fraction by $2, 3, 5, 7, ...$ etc. ✓ Continue until you can't go any further.
Example	**Simplify** $\frac{36}{48}$ To simplify $\frac{36}{48}$, find a number that both 36 and 48 are divisible by. Both are divisible by 12. Then: $\frac{36}{48} = \frac{36 \div 12}{48 \div 12} = \frac{3}{4}$

Your Turn!		
	1) $\frac{3}{15} = \frac{1}{5}$	2) $\frac{11}{55} = \frac{1}{5}$
	3) $\frac{12}{48} = \frac{1}{4}$	4) $\frac{11}{99} = \frac{1}{9}$
	5) $\frac{15}{75} = \frac{1}{5}$	6) $\frac{25}{100} = \frac{1}{4}$
	7) $\frac{16}{72} = \frac{2}{9}$	8) $\frac{32}{96} = \frac{1}{3}$
	9) $\frac{15}{65} = \frac{3}{13}$	10) $\frac{48}{92} = \frac{12}{23}$

Find more at

bit.ly/3nOGNko

Topic	**Adding and Subtracting Fractions**
Notes	✓ For "like" fractions (fractions with the same denominator), add or subtract the numerators and write the answer over the common denominator. ✓ Find equivalent fractions with the same denominator before you can add or subtract fractions with different denominators. ✓ Adding and Subtracting with the same denominator: $$\frac{a}{b} + \frac{c}{b} = \frac{a+c}{b} \;,\; \frac{a}{b} - \frac{c}{b} = \frac{a-c}{b}$$ ✓ Adding and Subtracting fractions with different denominators: $$\frac{a}{b} + \frac{c}{d} = \frac{ad + bc}{bd} \;,\; \frac{a}{b} - \frac{c}{d} = \frac{ad - bc}{bd}$$
Example	*Find the sum.* $\frac{3}{5} + \frac{2}{3} = \frac{(3)3+(5)(2)}{5 \times 3} = \frac{19}{15}$ *Subtract.* $\frac{4}{7} - \frac{3}{7} = \frac{1}{7}$

Your Turn!		
	1) $\frac{2}{3} + \frac{1}{5} =$	2) $\frac{8}{7} - \frac{3}{5} =$
	3) $\frac{4}{9} + \frac{5}{8} =$	4) $\frac{5}{8} - \frac{2}{5} =$
	5) $\frac{2}{5} + \frac{1}{6} =$	6) $\frac{2}{3} - \frac{1}{4} =$
Find more at bit.ly/3nKet2X	7) $\frac{8}{9} + \frac{5}{7} =$	8) $\frac{6}{7} - \frac{5}{9} =$

Topic	Adding and Subtracting Fractions - Answers
Notes	✓ For "like" fractions (fractions with the same denominator), add or subtract the numerators and write the answer over the common denominator. ✓ Find equivalent fractions with the same denominator before you can add or subtract fractions with different denominators. ✓ Adding and Subtracting with the same denominator: $$\frac{a}{b}+\frac{c}{b}=\frac{a+c}{b}, \quad \frac{a}{b}-\frac{c}{b}=\frac{a-c}{b}$$ ✓ Adding and Subtracting fractions with different denominators: $$\frac{a}{b}+\frac{c}{d}=\frac{ad+bc}{bd}, \quad \frac{a}{b}-\frac{c}{d}=\frac{ad-bc}{bd}$$
Example	*Find the sum.* $\frac{3}{5}+\frac{2}{3}=\frac{(3)3+(5)(2)}{5\times 3}=\frac{19}{15}$ *Subtract.* $\frac{4}{7}-\frac{3}{7}=\frac{1}{7}$
Your Turn! **Find more at** bit.ly/3nKet2X	1) $\frac{2}{3}+\frac{1}{5}=\frac{13}{15}$ 2) $\frac{8}{7}-\frac{3}{5}=\frac{19}{35}$ 3) $\frac{4}{9}+\frac{5}{8}=\frac{77}{72}$ 4) $\frac{5}{8}-\frac{2}{5}=\frac{9}{40}$ 5) $\frac{2}{5}+\frac{1}{6}=\frac{17}{30}$ 6) $\frac{2}{3}-\frac{1}{4}=\frac{5}{12}$ 7) $\frac{8}{9}+\frac{5}{7}=\frac{101}{63}$ 8) $\frac{6}{7}-\frac{5}{9}=\frac{19}{63}$

Topic	Multiplying and Dividing Fractions
Notes	✓ Multiplying fractions: multiply the top numbers and multiply the bottom numbers. ✓ Dividing fractions: Keep, Change, Flip Keep first fraction, change division sign to multiplication, and flip the numerator and denominator of the second fraction. Then, solve!
Examples	***Multiply.*** $\frac{2}{5} \times \frac{3}{4} =$ Multiply the top numbers and multiply the bottom numbers. $\frac{2}{5} \times \frac{3}{4} = \frac{2 \times 3}{5 \times 4} = \frac{6}{20}$, simplify: $\frac{6}{20} = \frac{6 \div 2}{20 \div 2} = \frac{3}{10}$ ***Divide.*** $\frac{2}{5} \div \frac{3}{4} =$ Keep first fraction, change division sign to multiplication, and flip the numerator and denominator of the second fraction. Then: $\frac{2}{5} \div \frac{3}{4} = \frac{2}{5} \times \frac{4}{3} = \frac{2 \times 4}{5 \times 3} = \frac{8}{15}$
Your Turn! **Find more at** bit.ly/3haSiQW	1) $\frac{3}{8} \times \frac{2}{5} =$ 　　　2) $\frac{4}{9} \div \frac{3}{4} =$ 3) $\frac{2}{7} \times \frac{3}{5} =$ 　　　4) $\frac{2}{5} \div \frac{7}{12} =$ 5) $\frac{1}{7} \times \frac{4}{9} =$ 　　　6) $\frac{2}{9} \div \frac{3}{7} =$ 7) $\frac{4}{7} \times \frac{3}{8} =$ 　　　8) $\frac{1}{6} \div \frac{3}{4} =$

Topic	**Multiplying and Dividing Fractions - Answers**
Notes	✓ Multiplying fractions: multiply the top numbers and multiply the bottom numbers. ✓ Dividing fractions: Keep, Change, Flip Keep first fraction, change division sign to multiplication, and flip the numerator and denominator of the second fraction. Then, solve!
Examples	**Multiply.** $\frac{2}{5} \times \frac{3}{4} =$ Multiply the top numbers and multiply the bottom numbers. $\frac{2}{5} \times \frac{3}{4} = \frac{2\times3}{5\times4} = \frac{6}{20}$, simplify: $\frac{6}{20} = \frac{6\div2}{20\div2} = \frac{3}{10}$ **Divide.** $\frac{2}{5} \div \frac{3}{4} =$ Keep first fraction, change division sign to multiplication, and flip the numerator and denominator of the second fraction. Then: $\frac{2}{5} \div \frac{3}{4} = \frac{2}{5} \times \frac{4}{3} = \frac{2\times4}{5\times3} = \frac{8}{15}$

Your Turn!		
	1) $\frac{3}{8} \times \frac{2}{5} = \frac{3}{20}$	2) $\frac{4}{9} \div \frac{3}{4} = \frac{16}{27}$
	3) $\frac{2}{7} \times \frac{3}{5} = \frac{6}{35}$	4) $\frac{2}{5} \div \frac{7}{12} = \frac{24}{35}$
	5) $\frac{1}{7} \times \frac{4}{9} = \frac{4}{63}$	6) $\frac{2}{9} \div \frac{3}{7} = \frac{14}{27}$
Find more at bit.ly/3haSiQW	7) $\frac{4}{7} \times \frac{3}{8} = \frac{3}{14}$	8) $\frac{1}{6} \div \frac{3}{4} = \frac{2}{9}$

Topic	**Adding Mixed Numbers**
Notes	Use the following steps for adding mixed numbers. ✓ Add whole numbers of the mixed numbers. ✓ Add the fractions of each mixed number. ✓ Find the Least Common Denominator (LCD) if necessary. ✓ Add whole numbers and fractions. ✓ Write your answer in lowest terms.
Example	***Add mixed numbers.*** $1\frac{1}{2} + 2\frac{2}{3} =$ Rewriting our equation with parts separated, $1 + \frac{1}{2} + 2 + \frac{2}{3}$ Add whole numbers: $1 + 2 = 3$ Add fractions: $\frac{1}{2} + \frac{2}{3} = \frac{3}{6} + \frac{4}{6} = \frac{7}{6} = 1\frac{1}{6}$, Now, combine the whole and fraction parts: $3 + 1 + \frac{1}{6} = 4\frac{1}{6}$

Your Turn!		
	1) $2\frac{1}{15} + 1\frac{2}{5} =$	2) $1\frac{3}{10} + 3\frac{1}{5} =$
	3) $1\frac{1}{10} + 2\frac{2}{5} =$	4) $2\frac{5}{6} + 2\frac{2}{9} =$
	5) $2\frac{2}{7} + 1\frac{2}{21} =$	6) $1\frac{3}{8} + 3\frac{2}{3} =$
Find more at bit.ly/2M4oAB	7) $1\frac{1}{6} + 4\frac{2}{7} =$	8) $2\frac{1}{6} + 1\frac{2}{5} =$

Topic	Adding Mixed Numbers - Answers
Notes	Use the following steps for adding mixed numbers. ✓ Add whole numbers of the mixed numbers. ✓ Add the fractions of each mixed number. ✓ Find the Least Common Denominator (LCD) if necessary. ✓ Add whole numbers and fractions. ✓ Write your answer in lowest terms.
Example	***Add mixed numbers.*** $1\frac{1}{2} + 2\frac{2}{3} =$ Rewriting our equation with parts separated, $1 + \frac{1}{2} + 2 + \frac{2}{3}$ Add whole numbers: $1 + 2 = 3$ Add fractions: $\frac{1}{2} + \frac{2}{3} = \frac{3}{6} + \frac{4}{6} = \frac{7}{6} = 1\frac{1}{6}$ Now, combine the whole and fraction parts: $3 + 1 + \frac{1}{6} = 4\frac{1}{6}$

Your Turn!		
	1) $2\frac{1}{15} + 1\frac{2}{5} = 3\frac{7}{15}$	2) $1\frac{3}{10} + 3\frac{1}{5} = 4\frac{1}{2}$
	3) $1\frac{1}{10} + 2\frac{2}{5} = 3\frac{1}{2}$	4) $2\frac{5}{6} + 2\frac{2}{9} = 5\frac{1}{18}$
	5) $2\frac{2}{7} + 1\frac{2}{21} = 3\frac{8}{21}$	6) $1\frac{3}{8} + 3\frac{2}{3} = 5\frac{1}{24}$
	7) $1\frac{1}{6} + 4\frac{2}{7} = 5\frac{19}{42}$	8) $2\frac{1}{6} + 1\frac{2}{5} = 3\frac{17}{30}$

Find more at

bit.ly/2M4oABB

Topic	**Subtracting Mixed Numbers**
Notes	Use the following steps for subtracting mixed numbers. ✓ Convert mixed numbers into improper fractions. $a\frac{c}{b} = \frac{ab+c}{b}$ ✓ Find equivalent fractions with the same denominator for unlike fractions (fractions with different denominators) ✓ Subtract the second fraction from the first one. ✓ Write your answer in lowest terms and convert it into a mixed number if the answer is an improper fraction.
Example	**Subtract.** $5\frac{1}{2} - 2\frac{2}{3} =$ Convert mixed numbers into fractions: $5\frac{1}{2} = \frac{5\times2+1}{2} = \frac{11}{2}$ and $2\frac{2}{3} = \frac{2\times3+2}{3} = \frac{8}{3}$, these two fractions are "unlike" fractions. (they have different denominators). Find equivalent fractions with the same denominator. Use this formula: $\frac{a}{b} - \frac{c}{d} = \frac{ad-bc}{bd}$ $\frac{11}{2} - \frac{8}{3} = \frac{(11)(3)-(2)(8)}{2\times3} = \frac{33-16}{6} = \frac{17}{6}$, the answer is an improper fraction, convert it into a mixed number. $\frac{17}{6} = 2\frac{5}{6}$
Your Turn! **Find more at** bit.ly/3aD3KDG	1) $3\frac{1}{4} - 1\frac{2}{3} =$ 2) $4\frac{4}{9} - 1\frac{1}{3} =$ 3) $6\frac{1}{4} - 1\frac{2}{7} =$ 4) $8\frac{2}{3} - 1\frac{1}{4} =$ 5) $8\frac{3}{4} - 1\frac{3}{8} =$ 6) $2\frac{3}{8} - 1\frac{2}{3} =$ 7) $8\frac{3}{5} - 1\frac{2}{25} =$ 8) $5\frac{2}{3} - 2\frac{4}{7} =$

Topic	**Subtracting Mixed Numbers - Answers**
Notes	Use the following steps for subtracting mixed numbers. ✓ Convert mixed numbers into improper fractions. $a\frac{c}{b} = \frac{ab+c}{b}$ ✓ Find equivalent fractions with the same denominator for unlike fractions (fractions with different denominators) ✓ Subtract the second fraction from the first one. ✓ Write your answer in lowest terms and convert it into a mixed number if the answer is an improper fraction.
Example	*Subtract.* $5\frac{1}{2} - 2\frac{2}{3} =$ Convert mixed numbers into fractions: $5\frac{1}{2} = \frac{5\times2+1}{2} = \frac{11}{2}$ and $2\frac{2}{3} = \frac{2\times3+2}{3} = \frac{8}{3}$, these two fractions are "unlike" fractions. (they have different denominators). Find equivalent fractions with the same denominator. Use this formula: $\frac{a}{b} - \frac{c}{d} = \frac{ad-bc}{bd}$ $\frac{11}{2} - \frac{8}{3} = \frac{(11)(3)-(2)(8)}{2\times3} = \frac{33-16}{6} = \frac{17}{6}$, the answer is an improper fraction, convert it into a mixed number. $\frac{17}{6} = 2\frac{5}{6}$

Your Turn!		
	1) $3\frac{1}{4} - 1\frac{2}{3} = 1\frac{7}{12}$	2) $4\frac{4}{9} - 1\frac{1}{3} = 3\frac{1}{9}$
	3) $6\frac{1}{4} - 1\frac{2}{7} = 4\frac{27}{28}$	4) $8\frac{2}{3} - 1\frac{1}{4} = 7\frac{5}{12}$
Find more at bit.ly/3aD3KDG	5) $8\frac{3}{4} - 1\frac{3}{8} = 7\frac{3}{8}$	6) $2\frac{3}{8} - 1\frac{2}{3} = \frac{17}{24}$
	7) $8\frac{3}{5} - 1\frac{2}{25} = 7\frac{13}{25}$	8) $5\frac{2}{3} - 2\frac{4}{7} = 3\frac{2}{21}$

Topic	**Multiplying Mixed Numbers**
Notes	✓ Convert the mixed numbers into fractions. $a\dfrac{c}{b} = a + \dfrac{c}{b} = \dfrac{ab + c}{b}$ ✓ Multiply fractions and simplify if necessary. $\dfrac{a}{b} \times \dfrac{c}{d} = \dfrac{a \times c}{b \times d}$ ✓ If the answer is an improper fraction (numerator is bigger than denominator), convert it into a mixed number.
Example	**Multiply** $2\dfrac{1}{4} \times 3\dfrac{1}{2}$ Convert mixed numbers into fractions: $2\dfrac{1}{4} = \dfrac{2 \times 4 + 1}{4} = \dfrac{9}{4}$ and $3\dfrac{1}{2} = \dfrac{3 \times 2 + 1}{2} = \dfrac{7}{2}$ Multiply two fractions: $\dfrac{9}{4} \times \dfrac{7}{2} = \dfrac{9 \times 7}{4 \times 2} = \dfrac{63}{8}$ The answer is an improper fraction. Convert it into a mixed number: $$\dfrac{63}{8} = 7\dfrac{7}{8}$$
Your Turn! **Find more at** bit.ly/3aPy7XJ	1) $3\dfrac{1}{3} \times 4\dfrac{1}{8} =$ 2) $5\dfrac{1}{2} \times 2\dfrac{6}{7} =$ 3) $3\dfrac{1}{3} \times 3\dfrac{3}{4} =$ 4) $2\dfrac{2}{9} \times 6\dfrac{1}{3} =$ 5) $2\dfrac{2}{7} \times 4\dfrac{3}{5} =$ 6) $1\dfrac{4}{7} \times 9\dfrac{1}{2} =$ 7) $3\dfrac{3}{5} \times 4\dfrac{1}{3} =$ 8) $5\dfrac{1}{4} \times 1\dfrac{1}{7} =$

Topic	Multiplying Mixed Numbers - Answers
Notes	✓ Convert the mixed numbers into fractions. $a\dfrac{c}{b} = a + \dfrac{c}{b} = \dfrac{ab + c}{b}$ ✓ Multiply fractions and simplify if necessary. $\dfrac{a}{b} \times \dfrac{c}{d} = \dfrac{a \times c}{b \times d}$ ✓ If the answer is an improper fraction (numerator is bigger than denominator), convert it into a mixed number.
Example	**Multiply** $2\dfrac{1}{4} \times 3\dfrac{1}{2}$ Convert mixed numbers into fractions: $2\dfrac{1}{4} = \dfrac{2 \times 4 + 1}{4} = \dfrac{9}{4}$ and $3\dfrac{1}{2} = \dfrac{3 \times 2 + 1}{2} = \dfrac{7}{2}$ Multiply two fractions: $\dfrac{9}{4} \times \dfrac{7}{2} = \dfrac{9 \times 7}{4 \times 2} = \dfrac{63}{8}$ The answer is an improper fraction. Convert it into a mixed number: $$\dfrac{63}{8} = 7\dfrac{7}{8}$$
Your Turn! **Find more at** bit.ly/3aPy7XJ	1) $3\dfrac{1}{3} \times 4\dfrac{1}{8} = 13\dfrac{3}{4}$ 2) $5\dfrac{1}{2} \times 2\dfrac{6}{7} = 15\dfrac{5}{7}$ 3) $3\dfrac{1}{3} \times 3\dfrac{3}{4} = 12\dfrac{1}{2}$ 4) $2\dfrac{2}{9} \times 6\dfrac{1}{3} = 14\dfrac{2}{27}$ 5) $2\dfrac{2}{7} \times 4\dfrac{3}{5} = 10\dfrac{18}{35}$ 6) $1\dfrac{4}{7} \times 9\dfrac{1}{2} = 14\dfrac{13}{14}$ 7) $3\dfrac{3}{5} \times 4\dfrac{1}{3} = 15\dfrac{3}{5}$ 8) $5\dfrac{1}{4} \times 1\dfrac{1}{7} = 6$

Topic	Dividing Mixed Numbers
Notes	✓ Convert the mixed numbers into improper fractions. $$a\frac{c}{b} = a + \frac{c}{b} = \frac{ab + c}{b}$$ ✓ Divide fractions and simplify if necessary.
Example	*Solve.* $2\frac{1}{3} \div 1\frac{1}{4} =$ Converting mixed numbers to fractions: $2\frac{1}{3} \div 1\frac{1}{4} = \frac{7}{3} \div \frac{5}{4}$ Keep, Change, Flip: $\frac{7}{3} \div \frac{5}{4} = \frac{7}{3} \times \frac{4}{5} = \frac{7 \times 4}{3 \times 5} = \frac{28}{15} = 1\frac{13}{15}$

Your Turn!	1) $2\frac{4}{7} \div 1\frac{1}{5} =$	2) $3\frac{3}{10} \div 2\frac{5}{8} =$
	3) $4\frac{2}{3} \div 3\frac{2}{5} =$	4) $5\frac{4}{5} \div 4\frac{3}{4} =$
	5) $1\frac{8}{9} \div 2\frac{3}{7} =$	6) $3\frac{3}{8} \div 2\frac{2}{5} =$
	7) $4\frac{1}{5} \div 3\frac{1}{9} =$	8) $4\frac{2}{3} \div 1\frac{8}{9} =$
Find more at bit.ly/2KLPk9k	9) $4\frac{1}{6} \div 3\frac{2}{3} =$	10) $6\frac{1}{3} \div 4\frac{1}{6} =$

Topic	Dividing Mixed Numbers- Answers
Notes	✓ Convert the mixed numbers into improper fractions. $$a\frac{c}{b} = a + \frac{c}{b} = \frac{ab + c}{b}$$ ✓ Divide fractions and simplify if necessary.
Example	**Solve.** $2\frac{1}{3} \div 1\frac{1}{4} =$ Converting mixed numbers to fractions: $2\frac{1}{3} \div 1\frac{1}{4} = \frac{7}{3} \div \frac{5}{4}$ Keep, Change, Flip: $\frac{7}{3} \div \frac{5}{4} = \frac{7}{3} \times \frac{4}{5} = \frac{7\times4}{3\times5} = \frac{28}{15} = 1\frac{13}{15}$

Your Turn!		
	1) $2\frac{4}{7} \div 1\frac{1}{5} = 2\frac{1}{7}$	2) $3\frac{3}{10} \div 2\frac{5}{8} = 1\frac{9}{35}$
	3) $4\frac{2}{3} \div 3\frac{2}{5} = 1\frac{19}{51}$	4) $5\frac{4}{5} \div 4\frac{3}{4} = 1\frac{21}{95}$
	5) $1\frac{8}{9} \div 2\frac{3}{7} = \frac{7}{9}$	6) $3\frac{3}{8} \div 2\frac{2}{5} = 1\frac{13}{32}$
	7) $4\frac{1}{5} \div 3\frac{1}{9} = 1\frac{7}{20}$	8) $4\frac{2}{3} \div 1\frac{8}{9} = 2\frac{8}{17}$
Find more at bit.ly/2KLPk9k	9) $4\frac{1}{6} \div 3\frac{2}{3} = 1\frac{3}{22}$	10) $6\frac{1}{3} \div 4\frac{1}{6} = 1\frac{13}{25}$

Topic	**Comparing Decimals**
Notes	Decimals: is a fraction written in a special form. For example, instead of writing $\frac{1}{2}$ you can write 0.5. For comparing decimals: ✓ Compare each digit of two decimals in the same place value. ✓ Start from left. Compare hundreds, tens, ones, tenth, hundredth, etc. ✓ To compare numbers, use these symbols: - Equal to =, Less than <, Greater than > Greater than or equal ≥, Less than or equal ≤
Examples	***Compare 0.40 and 0.04.*** 0.40 *is greater than* 0.04, because the tenth place of 0.40 is 4, but the tenth place of 0.04 is zero. Then: 0.40 > 0.04 ***Compare 0.0912 and 0.912.*** 0.912 *is greater than* 0.0912, because the tenth place of 0.912 is 9, but the tenth place of 0.0912 is zero. Then: 0.0912 < 0.912
Your Turn! **Find more at** bit.ly/2WHt2Za	1) 0.32 ☐ 0.36 2) 1.68 ☐ 1.70 3) 19.1 ☐ 19.09 4) 2.45 ☐ 2.089 5) 1.258 ☐ 12.58 6) 0.89 ☐ 0.890 7) 2.657 ☐ 3.568 8) 0.368 ☐ 0.683

Topic	Comparing Decimals – Answers
Notes	Decimals: is a fraction written in a special form. For example, instead of writing $\frac{1}{2}$ you can write 0.5. For comparing decimals: ✓ Compare each digit of two decimals in the same place value. ✓ Start from left. Compare hundreds, tens, ones, tenth, hundredth, etc. ✓ To compare numbers, use these symbols: - Equal to $=$, Less than $<$, Greater than $>$ Greater than or equal $\geq$, Less than or equal $\leq$
Examples	***Compare*** 0.40 ***and*** 0.04. 0.40 *is greater than* 0.04, because the tenth place of 0.40 is 4, but the tenth place of 0.04 is zero. Then: $0.40 > 0.04$ ***Compare*** 0.0912 ***and*** 0.912. 0.912 *is greater than* 0.0912, because the tenth place of 0.912 is 9, but the tenth place of 0.0912 is zero. Then: $0.0912 < 0.912$

Your Turn!	1) $0.32 < 0.36$	2) $1.68 < 1.70$
	3) $19.1 > 19.09$	4) $2.45 > 2.089$
	5) $1.258 < 12.58$	6) $0.89 = 0.890$
Find more at bit.ly/2WHt2Za	7) $2.657 < 3.568$	8) $0.368 < 0.683$

Topic	**Rounding Decimals**
Notes	✓ We can round decimals to a certain accuracy or number of decimal places. ✓ Let's review place values: For example: 35.4817 3: tens 5: ones 4: tenths 8: hundredths 1: thousandths 7:tens thousandths ✓ To round a decimal, find the place value you'll round to. ✓ Find the digit to the right of the place value you're rounding to. If it is 5 or bigger, add 1 to the place value you're rounding to and remove all digits on its right side. If the digit to the right of the place value is less than 5, keep the place value and remove all digits on the right.
Example	***Round 12.8365 to the hundredth place value.*** First look at the next place value to the right, (thousandths). It's 6 and it is greater than 5. Thus add 1 to the digit in the hundredth place. It is 3. $\rightarrow 3 + 1 = 4$, then, the answer is 12.84
Your Turn! **Find more at** bit.ly/3mKEIuf	***Round each number to the underlined place value.*** 1) 23.5<u>6</u>3= 2) 1.2<u>2</u>3= 3) 55.<u>4</u>23 = 4) 2<u>5</u>.62 = 5) 11.<u>2</u>65 = 6) 33.5<u>0</u>5 = 7) 4.4<u>8</u>3= 8) 9.0<u>1</u>8=

Topic	Rounding Decimals – Answers
Notes	✓ We can round decimals to a certain accuracy or number of decimal places. ✓ Let's review place values: For example: 35.4817 3: tens 5: ones 4: tenths 8: hundredths 1: thousandths 7: tens thousandths ✓ To round a decimal, find the place value you'll round to. ✓ Find the digit to the right of the place value you're rounding to. If it is 5 or bigger, add 1 to the place value you're rounding to and remove all digits on its right side. If the digit to the right of the place value is less than 5, keep the place value and remove all digits on the right.
Example	*Round 12.8365 to the hundredth place value.* First look at the next place value to the right, (thousandths). It's 6 and it is greater than 5. Thus add 1 to the digit in the hundredth place. It is 3. → $3 + 1 = 4$, then, the answer is 12.84
Your Turn! **Find more at** bit.ly/3mKEluf	*Round each number to the underlined place value.*

1) $23.56\underline{6}3 = 23.56$	2) $1.2\underline{2}3 = 1.22$
3) $55.\underline{4}23 = 55.4$	4) $2\underline{5}.62 = 26$
5) $11.\underline{2}65 = 11.3$	6) $33.5\underline{0}5 = 33.51$
7) $4.4\underline{8}3 = 4.48$	8) $9.0\underline{1}8 = 9.02$

Topic	Adding and Subtracting Decimals
Notes	✓ Line up the numbers. ✓ Add zeros to have same number of digits for both numbers if necessary. ✓ Add or subtract using column addition or subtraction.
Examples	***Add.*** $2.6 + 5.33 =$ First line up the numbers: $\begin{array}{r} 2.6 \\ + 5.33 \\ \hline \end{array}$ →Add zeros to have same number of digits for both numbers. $\begin{array}{r} 2.60 \\ + 5.33 \\ \hline \end{array}$ → Start with the hundredths place. $0 + 3 = 3$, $\begin{array}{r} 2.60 \\ + 5.33 \\ \hline 3 \end{array}$ → Continue with tenths place. $6 + 3 = 9$, $\begin{array}{r} 2.60 \\ + 5.33 \\ \hline .93 \end{array}$ → Add the ones place. $2 + 5 = 7$, $\begin{array}{r} 2.60 \\ + 5.33 \\ \hline 7.93 \end{array}$ ***Subtract.*** $4.79 - 3.13 =$ $\begin{array}{r} 4.79 \\ - 3.13 \\ \hline \end{array}$ Start with the hundredths place. $9 - 3 = 6$, $\begin{array}{r} 4.79 \\ - 3.13 \\ \hline 6 \end{array}$, continue with tenths place. $7 - 1 = 6$, $\begin{array}{r} 4.79 \\ - 3.13 \\ \hline .66 \end{array}$, subtract the ones place. $4 - 3 = 1$, $\begin{array}{r} 4.79 \\ - 3.13 \\ \hline 1.66 \end{array}$

Your Turn!	1) $28.15 + 16.58 =$	2) $65.36 - 56.16 =$
	3) $38.19 + 24.18 =$	4) $57.26 - 43.54 =$
Find more at bit.ly/38uyUdx	5) $21.67 + 37.91 =$	6) $39.58 - 26.44 =$

Topic	**Adding and Subtracting Decimals - Answers**
Notes	✓ Line up the numbers. ✓ Add zeros to have same number of digits for both numbers if necessary. ✓ Add or subtract using column addition or subtraction.
Examples	**Add.** $2.6 + 5.33 =$ First line up the numbers: $\begin{array}{r} 2.6 \\ +\,5.33 \\ \hline \end{array}$ →Add zeros to have same number of digits for both numbers. $\begin{array}{r} 2.60 \\ +\,5.33 \\ \hline \end{array}$ → Start with the hundredths place. $0 + 3 = 3$, $\begin{array}{r} 2.60 \\ +\,5.33 \\ \hline 3 \end{array}$ → Continue with tenths place. $6 + 3 = 9$, $\begin{array}{r} 2.60 \\ +\,5.33 \\ \hline .93 \end{array}$ → Add the ones place. $2 + 5 = 7$, $\begin{array}{r} 2.60 \\ +\,5.33 \\ \hline 7.93 \end{array}$ **Subtract.** $4.79 - 3.13 =$ $\begin{array}{r} 4.79 \\ -\,3.13 \\ \hline \end{array}$ Start with the hundredths place. $9 - 3 = 6$, $\begin{array}{r} 4.79 \\ -\,3.13 \\ \hline 6 \end{array}$, continue with tenths place. $7 - 1 = 6$, $\begin{array}{r} 4.79 \\ -\,3.13 \\ \hline .66 \end{array}$, subtract the ones place. $4 - 3 = 1$, $\begin{array}{r} 4.79 \\ -\,3.13 \\ \hline 1.66 \end{array}$
Your Turn! **Find more at** bit.ly/38uyUdx	1) $28.15 + 16.58 = 44.73$ 2) $65.36 - 56.16 = 9.20$ 3) $38.19 + 24.18 = 62.37$ 4) $57.26 - 43.54 = 13.72$ 5) $21.67 + 37.91 = 59.58$ 6) $39.58 - 26.44 = 13.14$

Topic	**Multiplying and Dividing Decimals**
Notes	For Multiplication: ✓ Ignore the decimal point and set up and multiply the numbers as you do with whole numbers. ✓ Count the total number of decimal places in both factors. ✓ Place the decimal point in the product. For Division: ✓ If the divisor is not a whole number, move decimal point to right to make it a whole number. Do the same for dividend. ✓ Divide similar to whole numbers.
Examples	***Find the product.*** $1.2 \times 2.3 =$ Set up and multiply the numbers as you do with whole numbers. Line up the numbers: $\overset{12}{\underset{}{\times 23}}$ → Multiply: $\overset{12}{\underset{276}{\times 23}}$ → Count the total number of decimal places in both of the factors. There are two decimal digits. Then: $1.2 \times 2.3 = 2.76$ ***Find the quotient.*** $5.6 \div 0.8 =$ The divisor is not a whole number. Multiply it by 10 to get 8. → $0.8 \times 10 = 8$ Do the same for the dividend to get 56 → $5.6 \times 10 = 56$ Now, divide: $56 \div 8 = 7$. The answer is 7.
Your Turn! **Find more at** bit.ly/34DZ0cS	1) $1.16 \times 0.5 =$ 2) $45.5 \div 5 =$

Topic	Multiplying and Dividing Decimals – Answers
Notes	For Multiplication: ✓ Ignore the decimal point and set up and multiply the numbers as you do with whole numbers. ✓ Count the total number of decimal places in both factors. ✓ Place the decimal point in the product. For Division: ✓ If the divisor is not a whole number, move decimal point to right to make it a whole number. Do the same for dividend. ✓ Divide similar to whole numbers.
Examples	***Find the product.*** $1.2 \times 2.3 =$ Set up and multiply the numbers as you do with whole numbers. Line up the numbers: $\frac{\overset{12}{\times 23}}{}$ → Multiply: $\frac{\overset{12}{\times 23}}{276}$ → Count the total number of decimal places in both of the factors. There are two decimal digits. Then: $1.2 \times 2.3 = 2.76$ ***Find the quotient.*** $5.6 \div 0.8 =$ The divisor is not a whole number. Multiply it by 10 to get 8. → $0.8 \times 10 = 8$ Do the same for the dividend to get 56 → $5.6 \times 10 = 56$ Now, divide: $56 \div 8 = 7$. The answer is 7.
Your Turn! **Find more at** bit.ly/34DZ0cS 	1) $1.16 \times 0.5 = 0.58$ 2) $45.5 \div 5 = 9.1$ 3) $0.9 \times 0.68 = 0.612$ 4) $66.8 \div 0.2 = 334$ 5) $0.16 \times 0.4 = 0.064$ 6) $58.9 \div 100 = 0.589$

Topic	Adding and Subtracting Integers
Notes	✓ Integers include: zero, counting numbers, and the negative of the counting numbers. $\{..., -3, -2, -1, 0, 1, 2, 3, ...\}$ ✓ Add a positive integer by moving to the right on the number line. ✓ Add a negative integer by moving to the left on the number line. Subtract an integer by adding its opposite.
Examples	***Solve.*** $(4) - (-8) =$ Keep the first number and convert the sign of the second number to its opposite. (change subtraction into addition. Then: $(4) + 8 = 12$ ***Solve.*** $42 + (12 - 26) =$ First subtract the numbers in brackets, $12 - 26 = -14$ Then: $42 + (-14) = \rightarrow$ change addition into subtraction: $42 - 14 = 28$

Your Turn!	1) $-(13) + 10 =$	2) $(-6) + (-11) + 15 =$
	3) $(-13) + 7 =$	4) $3 - (-7) + 14 =$
	5) $(-7) + (-8) =$	6) $16 - (-4 + 8) =$
Find more at bit.ly/3aKx5vl	7) $2 + (-6) + 8 =$	8) $-(19) - (-6) + 3 =$

Topic	Adding and Subtracting Integers – Answers
Notes	✓ Integers include: zero, counting numbers, and the negative of the counting numbers. $\{..., -3, -2, -1, 0, 1, 2, 3, ...\}$ ✓ Add a positive integer by moving to the right on the number line. ✓ Add a negative integer by moving to the left on the number line. Subtract an integer by adding its opposite.
Examples	**Solve**. $(4) - (-8) =$ Keep the first number and convert the sign of the second number to its opposite. (change subtraction into addition. Then: $(4) + 8 = 12$ **Solve.** $42 + (12 - 26) =$ First subtract the numbers in brackets, $12 - 26 = -14$ Then: $42 + (-14) = \ \rightarrow$ change addition into subtraction: $42 - 14 = 28$

Your Turn! **Find more at** bit.ly/3aKx5vI		
	1) $-(13) + 10 = -3$	2) $(-6) + (-11) + 15 = -2$
	3) $(-13) + 7 = -6$	4) $3 - (-7) + 14 = 24$
	5) $(-7) + (-8) = -15$	6) $16 - (-4 + 8) = 12$
	7) $2 + (-6) + 8 = 4$	8) $-(19) - (-6) + 3 = -10$

Topic	**Multiplying and Dividing Integers**
Notes	Use following rules for multiplying and dividing integers: ✓ (negative) × (negative) = positive ✓ (negative) ÷ (negative) = positive ✓ (negative) × (positive) = negative ✓ (negative) ÷ (positive) = negative ✓ (positive) × (positive) = positive ✓ (positive) ÷ (negative) = negative
Examples	*Solve.* $2 \times (14 - 17) =$ First subtract the numbers in brackets, $14 - 17 = -3 \rightarrow (2) \times (-3) =$ Now use this rule: (positive) × (negative) = negative $(2) \times (-3) = -6$ *Solve.* $(-7) + (-36 \div 4) =$ First divide -36 by 4, the numbers in brackets, using this rule: (negative) ÷ (positive) = negative Then: $-36 \div 4 = -9$. Now, add -7 and -9: $(-7) + (-9) = -7 - 9 = -16$

Your Turn!	1) $(-4) \times 3 =$	2) $(-48) \div (-8) =$
	3) $(-11) \times (-3) =$	4) $81 \div (-9) =$
	5) $(15 - 12) \times (-7) =$	6) $(-12) \div (3) =$
Find more at bit.ly/3pjQW98	7) $3 \times (-7) =$	8) $(9) \div (-3) =$

Topic	**Multiplying and Dividing Integers - Answers**
Notes	Use following rules for multiplying and dividing integers: ✓ (negative) × (negative) = positive ✓ (negative) ÷ (negative) = positive ✓ (negative) × (positive) = negative ✓ (negative) ÷ (positive) = negative ✓ (positive) × (positive) = positive ✓ (positive) ÷ (negative) = negative
Examples	***Solve.*** $2 \times (14 - 17) =$ First subtract the numbers in brackets, $14 - 17 = -3 \rightarrow (2) \times (-3) =$ Now use this rule: (positive) × (negative) = negative $(2) \times (-3) = -6$ ***Solve.*** $(-7) + (-36 \div 4) =$ First divide -36 by 4, the numbers in brackets, using this rule: (negative) ÷ (positive) = negative Then: $-36 \div 4 = -9$. Now, add -7 and -9: $(-7) + (-9) = -7 - 9 = -16$

Your Turn!		
	1) $(-4) \times 3 = -12$	2) $(-48) \div (-8) = 6$
	3) $(-11) \times (-3) = 33$	4) $81 \div (-9) = -9$
Find more at bit.ly/3pjQW98	5) $(15 - 12) \times (-7) =$ -21	6) $(-12) \div (3) = -4$
	7) $3 \times (-7) = -21$	8) $(9) \div (-3) = -3$

Topic	Order of Operation
Notes	When there is more than one math operation, use PEMDAS: (to memorize this rule, remember the phrase "Please Excuse My Dear Aunt Sally") ✓ Parentheses ✓ Exponents ✓ Multiplication and Division (from left to right) ✓ Addition and Subtraction (from left to right)
Examples	***Calculate.*** $(18 - 26) \div (2^4 \div 4) =$ First simplify inside parentheses: $(-8) \div (16 \div 4) = (-8) \div (4)$ Then: $(-8) \div (4) = -2$ ***Solve.*** $(-5 \times 7) - (18 - 3^2) =$ First calculate within parentheses: $(-5 \times 7) - (18 - 3^2) = (-35) - (18 - 9)$ Then: $(-35) - (18 - 9) = -35 - 9 = -44$

Your Turn!	1) $(12 \times 3) \div (6 + 6) =$	2) $(36 \div 4) + (11 - 4) =$
	3) $(-9) + (5 \times 6) + 14 =$	4) $(-10 \times 5) \div (2^2 + 1) =$
	5) $[-16(32 \div 2^3)] \div 8 =$	6) $(-7) + (72 \div 3^2) + 12 =$
Find more at bit.ly/37LBw7X	7) $[10(64 \div 2^4)] - 3^2 =$	8) $3^3 + (-6 \times 2^3) + 4 =$

Topic	**Order of Operation – Answers**
Notes	When there is more than one math operation, use PEMDAS: (to memorize this rule, remember the phrase "Please Excuse My Dear Aunt Sally") ✓ Parentheses ✓ Exponents ✓ Multiplication and Division (from left to right) ✓ Addition and Subtraction (from left to right)
Examples	***Calculate.*** $(18 - 26) \div (2^4 \div 4) =$ First simplify inside parentheses: $(-8) \div (16 \div 4) = (-8) \div (4)$ Then: $(-8) \div (4) = -2$ ***Solve.*** $(-5 \times 7) - (18 - 3^2) =$ First calculate within parentheses: $(-5 \times 7) - (18 - 3^2) = (-35) - (18 - 9)$ Then: $(-35) - (18 - 9) = -35 - 9 = -44$

Your Turn!		
	1) $(12 \times 3) \div (6 + 6) = 3$	2) $(36 \div 4) + (11 - 4) = 16$
	3) $(-9) + (5 \times 6) + 14 = 35$	4) $(-10 \times 5) \div (2^2 + 1) = -10$
	5) $[-16(32 \div 2^3)] \div 8 = -8$	6) $(-7) + (72 \div 3^2) + 12 = 13$
	7) $[10(64 \div 2^4)] - 3^2 =$ 31	8) $3^3 + (-6 \times 2^3) + 4 = -17$

Find more at

bit.ly/37LBw7X

Topic	Integers and Absolute Value
Notes	✓ The absolute value of a number is its distance from zero, in either direction, on the number line. For example, the distance of 9 and -9 from zero on number line is 9. ✓ Absolute value is symbolized by vertical bars, as in $\lvert x \rvert$.
Example	***Calculate.*** $\lvert 8 - 5 \rvert \times \lvert 12 - 16 \rvert =$ First calculate $\lvert 8 - 5 \rvert$, $\rightarrow \lvert 8 - 5 \rvert = \lvert 3 \rvert$, the absolute value of 3 is 3, $\lvert 3 \rvert = 3$ $8 \times \lvert 12 - 16 \rvert =$ Now calculate $\lvert 12 - 16 \rvert$, $\rightarrow \lvert 12 - 16 \rvert = \lvert -4 \rvert$, the absolute value of -4 is 4, $\lvert -4 \rvert = 4$. Then: $3 \times 4 = 12$

Your Turn!		
	1) $12 - \lvert 6 - 15 \rvert =$	2) $12 - \lvert 14 - 18 \rvert - \lvert 6 \rvert =$
	3) $\lvert 21 \rvert - \dfrac{\lvert -25 \rvert}{5} =$	4) $\lvert 30 \rvert + \dfrac{\lvert -49 \rvert}{7} =$
	5) $\dfrac{\lvert 7 \times -8 \rvert}{4} \times \dfrac{\lvert -12 \rvert}{2} =$	6) $\dfrac{\lvert 10 \times -6 \rvert}{5} \times \lvert -9 \rvert =$
Find more at bit.ly/3aD521u	7) $\dfrac{\lvert -45 \rvert}{9} \times \dfrac{\lvert -42 \rvert}{7} =$	8) $\lvert -25 + 4 \rvert \times \dfrac{\lvert -8 \times 3 \rvert}{6} =$

Topic	Integers and Absolute Value – Answers
Notes	✓ The absolute value of a number is its distance from zero, in either direction, on the number line. For example, the distance of 9 and -9 from zero on number line is 9. ✓ Absolute value is symbolized by vertical bars, as in $\lvert x \rvert$.
Example	***Calculate.*** $\lvert 8 - 5 \rvert \times \lvert 12 - 16 \rvert =$ First calculate $\lvert 8 - 5 \rvert$, $\rightarrow \lvert 8 - 5 \rvert = \lvert 3 \rvert$, the absolute value of 3 is 3, $\lvert 3 \rvert = 3$ $8 \times \lvert 12 - 16 \rvert =$ Now calculate $\lvert 12 - 16 \rvert$, $\rightarrow \lvert 12 - 16 \rvert = \lvert -4 \rvert$, the absolute value of -4 is 4, $\lvert -4 \rvert = 4$. Then: $3 \times 4 = 12$

Your Turn!		
	1) $12 - \lvert 6 - 15 \rvert = 3$	2) $12 - \lvert 14 - 18 \rvert - \lvert 6 \rvert = 2$
	3) $\lvert 21 \rvert - \dfrac{\lvert -25 \rvert}{5} = 16$	4) $\lvert 30 \rvert + \dfrac{\lvert -49 \rvert}{7} = 37$
	5) $\dfrac{\lvert 7 \times -8 \rvert}{4} \times \dfrac{\lvert -12 \rvert}{2} = 84$	6) $\dfrac{\lvert 10 \times -6 \rvert}{5} \times \lvert -9 \rvert = 108$
Find more at bit.ly/3aD521u	7) $\dfrac{\lvert -45 \rvert}{9} \times \dfrac{\lvert -42 \rvert}{7} = 30$	8) $\lvert -25 + 4 \rvert \times \dfrac{\lvert -8 \times 3 \rvert}{6} = 84$

Topic	**Simplifying Ratios**
Notes	✓ Ratios are used to make comparisons between two numbers. ✓ Ratios can be written as a fraction, using the word "to", or with a colon. ✓ You can calculate equivalent ratios by multiplying or dividing both sides of the ratio by the same number.
Examples	***Simplify.*** $18:63 =$ Both numbers 18 and 63 are divisible by $9 \Rightarrow 18 \div 9 = 2, 63 \div 9 = 7$, Then: $18:63 = 2:7$ ***Simplify.*** $\frac{25}{45} =$ Both numbers 25 and 45 are divisible by 5, $\Rightarrow 25 \div 5 = 5, 45 \div 5 = 9$, Then: $\frac{25}{45} = \frac{5}{9}$

Your Turn!	1) $\frac{6}{48} = -$	2) $\frac{35}{60} = -$
	3) $\frac{15}{35} = -$	4) $\frac{42}{54} = -$
	5) $\frac{12}{36} = -$	6) $\frac{30}{80} = -$
Find more at bit.ly/3nKwq0Z	7) $\frac{16}{36} = -$	8) $\frac{30}{108} = -$

Topic	Simplifying Ratios – Answers
Notes	✓ Ratios are used to make comparisons between two numbers. ✓ Ratios can be written as a fraction, using the word "to", or with a colon. ✓ You can calculate equivalent ratios by multiplying or dividing both sides of the ratio by the same number.
Examples	***Simplify.*** $18:63 =$ Both numbers 18 and 63 are divisible by $9 \Rightarrow 18 \div 9 = 2, 63 \div 9 = 7$, Then: $18:63 = 2:7$ ***Simplify.*** $\dfrac{25}{45} =$ Both numbers 25 and 45 are divisible by 5, $\Rightarrow 25 \div 5 = 5, 45 \div 5 = 9$, Then: $\dfrac{25}{45} = \dfrac{5}{9}$
Your Turn! **Find more at** bit.ly/3nKwq0Z	1) $\dfrac{6}{48} = \dfrac{1}{8}$ 2) $\dfrac{35}{60} = \dfrac{7}{12}$ 3) $\dfrac{15}{35} = \dfrac{3}{7}$ 4) $\dfrac{42}{54} = \dfrac{7}{9}$ 5) $\dfrac{12}{36} = \dfrac{1}{3}$ 6) $\dfrac{30}{80} = \dfrac{3}{8}$ 7) $\dfrac{16}{36} = \dfrac{4}{9}$ 8) $\dfrac{30}{108} = \dfrac{5}{18}$

Topic	**Proportional Ratios**
Notes	✓ Two ratios are proportional if they represent the same relationship. ✓ A proportion means that two ratios are equal. It can be written in two ways: $\frac{a}{b} = \frac{c}{d}$ $a : b = c : d$
Example	*Solve this proportion for* x. $\frac{5}{8} = \frac{35}{x}$ Use cross multiplication: $\frac{5}{8} = \frac{35}{x} \Rightarrow 5 \times x = 8 \times 35 \Rightarrow 5x = 280$ Divide to find x: $x = \frac{280}{5} \Rightarrow x = 56$

Your Turn!	1) $\frac{1}{3} = \frac{7}{x} \Rightarrow x = $ ____	2) $\frac{4}{3} = \frac{20}{x} \Rightarrow x = $ ____
	3) $\frac{3}{11} = \frac{6}{x} \Rightarrow x = $ ____	4) $\frac{12}{20} = \frac{x}{200} \Rightarrow x = $ ____
	5) $\frac{9}{12} = \frac{27}{x} \Rightarrow x = $ ____	6) $\frac{14}{16} = \frac{x}{80} \Rightarrow x = $ ____
Find more at bit.ly/37GHQxp	7) $\frac{5}{14} = \frac{40}{x} \Rightarrow x = $ ____	8) $\frac{8}{12} = \frac{36}{x} \Rightarrow x = $ ____

Topic	**Proportional Ratios - Answers**
Notes	✓ Two ratios are proportional if they represent the same relationship. ✓ A proportion means that two ratios are equal. It can be written in two ways: $\dfrac{a}{b} = \dfrac{c}{d}$ $\qquad\qquad a : b = c : d$
Example	*Solve this proportion for* x. $\dfrac{5}{8} = \dfrac{35}{x}$ Use cross multiplication: $\dfrac{5}{8} = \dfrac{35}{x} \Rightarrow 5 \times x = 8 \times 35 \Rightarrow 5x = 280$ Divide to find x: $\quad x = \dfrac{280}{5} \Rightarrow x = 56$

Your Turn!		
	1) $\dfrac{1}{3} = \dfrac{7}{x} \Rightarrow x = 21$	2) $\dfrac{4}{3} = \dfrac{20}{x} \Rightarrow x = 15$
	3) $\dfrac{3}{11} = \dfrac{6}{x} \Rightarrow x = 22$	4) $\dfrac{12}{20} = \dfrac{x}{200} \Rightarrow x = 120$
	5) $\dfrac{9}{12} = \dfrac{27}{x} \Rightarrow x = 36$	6) $\dfrac{14}{16} = \dfrac{x}{80} \Rightarrow x = 70$
Find more at bit.ly/37GHQxp	7) $\dfrac{5}{14} = \dfrac{40}{x} \Rightarrow x = 112$	8) $\dfrac{8}{12} = \dfrac{36}{x} \Rightarrow x = 54$

Topic	**Create Proportion**
Notes	✓ To create a proportion, simply find (or create) two equal fractions. ✓ Use cross products to solve proportions or to test whether two ratios are equal and form a proportion. $\frac{a}{b} = \frac{c}{d} \Rightarrow a \times d = c \times b$
Example	***State if this pair of ratios form a proportion.*** $\frac{2}{3}$ *and* $\frac{12}{30}$ Use cross multiplication: $\frac{2}{3} = \frac{12}{30} \rightarrow 2 \times 30 = 12 \times 3 \rightarrow 60 = 36$, which is not correct. Therefore, this pair of ratios doesn't form a proportion.
Your Turn!	***State if each pair of ratios form a proportion.*** 1) $\frac{3}{5}$ and $\frac{24}{45}$ 2) $\frac{4}{9}$ and $\frac{16}{24}$ 3) $\frac{3}{11}$ and $\frac{9}{33}$ 4) $\frac{7}{10}$ and $\frac{14}{20}$ 5) $\frac{7}{9}$ and $\frac{48}{81}$ 6) $\frac{6}{8}$ and $\frac{12}{14}$ 7) $\frac{2}{10}$ and $\frac{6}{30}$ 8) $\frac{3}{18}$ and $\frac{19}{28}$ 9) Solve. Five pencils costs \$0.50. How many pencils can you buy for \$2.50? _____

Find more at

bit.ly/37GHQxp

Topic	Create Proportion – Answers
Notes	✓ To create a proportion, simply find (or create) two equal fractions. ✓ Use cross products to solve proportions or to test whether two ratios are equal and form a proportion. $\frac{a}{b} = \frac{c}{d} \Rightarrow a \times d = c \times b$
Example	***State if this pair of ratios form a proportion.*** $\frac{2}{3}$ *and* $\frac{12}{30}$ Use cross multiplication: $\frac{2}{3} = \frac{12}{30} \rightarrow 2 \times 30 = 12 \times 3 \rightarrow 60 = 36$, which is not correct. Therefore, this pair of ratios doesn't form a proportion.

Your Turn!	***State if each pair of ratios form a proportion.***

1) $\frac{3}{5}$ and $\frac{24}{45}$, *No*	2) $\frac{4}{9}$ and $\frac{16}{24}$, *No*
3) $\frac{3}{11}$ and $\frac{9}{33}$, *Yes*	4) $\frac{7}{10}$ and $\frac{14}{20}$, *Yes*
5) $\frac{7}{9}$ and $\frac{48}{81}$, *No*	6) $\frac{6}{8}$ and $\frac{12}{14}$, *No*
7) $\frac{2}{10}$ and $\frac{6}{30}$, *Yes*	8) $\frac{3}{18}$ and $\frac{19}{28}$, *No*

Find more at

bit.ly/37GHQxp

9) Solve.

Five pencils costs $0.50. How many pencils can you buy for $2.50? 5 pencils

Topic	**Similarity and Ratios**
Notes	✓ Two figures are similar if they have the same shape. ✓ Two or more figures are similar if the corresponding angles are equal, and the corresponding sides are in proportion.
Example	*Following triangles are similar. What is the value of unknown side?* **Solution:** Find the corresponding sides and write a proportion: $\frac{4}{12} = \frac{x}{9}$. Now, use cross product to solve for x: $\frac{4}{12} = \frac{x}{9} \rightarrow 4 \times 9 = 12 \times x \rightarrow 36 = 12x$. Divide both sides by 12. Then: $12x = 36 \rightarrow \frac{36}{12} = \frac{12x}{12} \rightarrow x = 3$. The missing side is 3.

Your Turn!

1)

2)

3)

4)

5)

6)

Topic	**Similarity and Ratios - Answers**
Notes	✓ Two figures are similar if they have the same shape. ✓ Two or more figures are similar if the corresponding angles are equal, and the corresponding sides are in proportion.
Example	*Following triangles are similar. What is the value of unknown side?* **Solution:** Find the corresponding sides and write a proportion: $\frac{4}{12} = \frac{x}{9}$. Now, use cross product to solve for x: $\frac{4}{12} = \frac{x}{9} \rightarrow 4 \times 9 = 12 \times x \rightarrow 36 = 12x$. Divide both sides by 12. Then: $12x = 36 \rightarrow \frac{36}{12} = \frac{12x}{12} \rightarrow x = 3$. The missing side is 3.

Your Turn!

1) 10

2) 11

3) 4

4) 8

5) 10

6) 9

Find more at

bit.ly/2KKKmcV

Topic	Percent Problems

Notes	✓ In each percent problem, we are looking for the base, or part or the percent.
	✓ Use the following equations to find each missing section.
	   o Base = Part ÷ Percent
	   o Part = Percent × Base
	   o Percent = Part ÷ Base

Examples	**18 *is what percent of* 30?** In this problem, we are looking for the percent. Use the following equation: $Percent = Part \div Base \rightarrow Percent = 18 \div 30 = 0.6 = 60\%$ **40 *is* 20% *of what number?*** Use the following formula: $Base = Part \div Percent \rightarrow Base = 40 \div 0.20 = 200$ 40 is 20% of 200.

Your Turn!		
	1) What is 20 percent of 500?	2) 24 is what percent of 160?
	3) 60 is 5 percent of what number?	4) 48 is what percent of 300?
	5) 84 is 28 percent of what number?	6) 63 is what percent of 700?
Find more at bit.ly/34Gy3FL	7) 63 is 21 percent of what number?	8) 42 is what percent of 600?

Topic	Percent Problems – Answers
Notes	✓ In each percent problem, we are looking for the base, or part or the percent. ✓ Use the following equations to find each missing section. ○ Base = Part ÷ Percent ○ Part = Percent × Base ○ Percent = Part ÷ Base
Examples	**18 *is what percent of* 30?** In this problem, we are looking for the percent. Use the following equation: $Percent = Part \div Base \rightarrow Percent = 18 \div 30 = 0.6 = 60\%$ **40 *is* 20% *of what number?*** Use the following formula: $Base = Part \div Percent \rightarrow Base = 40 \div 0.20 = 200$ 40 is 20% of 200.

Your Turn!		
Find more at bit.ly/34Gy3FL 	1) What is 20 percent of 500? 100	2) 24 is what percent of 160? 15%
	3) 60 is 5 percent of what number? 1,200	4) 48 is what percent of 300? 16%
	5) 84 is 28 percent of what number? 300	6) 63 is what percent of 700? 9%
	7) 63 is 21 percent of what number? 300	8) 42 is what percent of 600? 7%

Topic	Percent of Increase and Decrease
Notes	✓ Percent of change (increase or decrease) is a mathematical concept that represents the degree of change over time. ✓ To find the percentage of increase or decrease: 1- New Number – Original Number 2- The result ÷ Original Number × 100 Or use this formula: Percent of change = $\dfrac{new\ number\ -\ original\ number}{original\ number} \times 100$
Example	The price of a printer increases from \$40 to \$50. What is the percent increase? **Solution:** Percent of change = $\dfrac{new\ number\ -\ original\ number}{original\ number} \times 100 =$ $\dfrac{50\ -\ 40}{40} \times 100 = 25$ The percentage increase is 25. It means that the price of the printer increased 25%.
Your Turn! **Find more at** bit.ly/3pgPQes	1) In a class, the number of students has been increased from 30 to 33. What is the percentage increase? _____ % 2) The price of gasoline rose from \$4.60 to \$4.83 in one month. By what percent did the gas price rise? _____ % 3) A shirt was originally priced at \$60.00. It went on sale for \$54.00. What was the percent that the shirt was discounted? _____ % 4) Jason got a raise, and his hourly wage increased from \$40 to \$56. What is the percent increase? _____ % *cross multiply*

Topic	Percent of Increase and Decrease – Answers
Notes	✓ Percent of change (increase or decrease) is a mathematical concept that represents the degree of change over time. ✓ To find the percentage of increase or decrease: 1- New Number – Original Number 2- The result ÷ Original Number × 100 Or use this formula: Percent of change $= \dfrac{new\ number\ -\ original\ number}{original\ number} \times 100$
Example	The price of a printer increases from \$40 to \$50. What is the percent increase? **Solution:** Percent of change $= \dfrac{new\ number\ -\ original\ number}{original\ number} \times 100 = \dfrac{50\ -\ 40}{40} \times 100 =$ 25 The percentage increase is 25. It means that the price of the printer increased 25%.
Your Turn! **Find more at** bit.ly/3pgPQes 	1) In a class, the number of students has been increased from 30 to 33. What is the percentage increase? 10%
	2) The price of gasoline rose from \$4.60 to \$4.83 in one month. By what percent did the gas price rise? 5%
	3) A shirt was originally priced at \$60.00. It went on sale for \$54.00. What was the percent that the shirt was discounted? -−10%
	4) Jason got a raise, and his hourly wage increased from \$40 to \$56. What is the percent increase? 40%

Tax= +
Discount-subtract   *tip= +*

Topic	Discount, Tax and Tip
Notes	✓ Discount = Multiply the regular price by the rate of discount ✓ Selling price = original price – discount ✓ To find tax, multiply the tax rate to the taxable amount (income, property value, etc.) ✓ To find tip, multiply the rate to the selling price.
Example	The original price of a table is $300 and the tax rate is 6%. What is the final price of the table? **Solution:** First find the tax amount. To find tax: Multiply the tax rate to the taxable amount. Tax rate is 6% or 0.06. Then: $0.06 \times 300 = 18$. The tax amount is $18. Final price is: $300 + $18 = $318

Your Turn!		
	1) Original price of a chair: $350 Tax: 12%, Selling price: _____	2) Original price of a computer: $600 Discount: 15%, Selling price: _____
	3) Original price of a printer: $250 Tax: 10%, Selling price: _____	4) Original price of a sofa: $620 Discount: 25%, Selling price: _____
	5) Original price of a mattress: $800 Tax: 12%, Selling price: _____	6) Original price of a book: $150 Discount: 60%, Selling price: _____
Find more at bit.ly/2Je5lo0	7) Restaurant bill: $24.00 Tip: 25%, Final amount: _____	8) Restaurant bill: $80.00 Tip: 15%, Final amount: _____

Topic	Discount, Tax and Tip – Answers
Notes	✓ Discount = Multiply the regular price by the rate of discount ✓ Selling price = original price – discount ✓ To find tax, multiply the tax rate to the taxable amount (income, property value, etc.) ✓ To find tip, multiply the rate to the selling price.
Example	*The original price of a table is $300 and the tax rate is 6%. What is the final price of the table?* **Solution:** First find the tax amount. To find tax: Multiply the tax rate to the taxable amount. Tax rate is 6% or 0.06. Then: $0.06 \times 300 = 18$. The tax amount is $18. Final price is: $300 + $18 = $318

Your Turn!	1) Original price of a chair: $350 Tax: 12%, Selling price: $392	2) Original price of a computer: $600 Discount: 15%, Selling price: $510
	3) Original price of a printer: $250 Tax: 10%, Selling price: $275	4) Original price of a sofa: $620 Discount: 25%, Selling price: $465
	5) Original price of a mattress: $800 Tax: 12%, Selling price: $896	6) Original price of a book: $150 Discount: 60%, Selling price: $60
Find more at bit.ly/2Je5lo0 	7) Restaurant bill: $24.00 Tip: 25%, Final amount: $30	8) Restaurant bill: $80.00 Tip: 15%, Final amount: $92

Topic	Simple Interest
Notes	✓ Simple Interest: The charge for borrowing money or the return for lending it. To solve a simple interest problem, use this formula: Interest = principal x rate x time $\Rightarrow$ $I = p \times r \times t$
Example	*Find simple interest for* $3,000$ *investment at* 5% *for 4 years.* **Solution:** Use Interest formula: $I = prt$ ($P = \$3{,}000$, $r = 5\% = 0.05$ and $t = 4$) Then: $I = 3{,}000 \times 0.05 \times 4 = \$600$

Your Turn!		
	1) \$200 at 3% for 2 years. Simple interest: \$_____	2) \$4,200 at 4% for 5 years. Simple interest: \$_____
	3) \$720 at 2% for 5 years. Simple interest: \$_____	4) \$2,200 at 8% for 4 years. Simple interest: \$_____
	5) \$1,800 at 3% for 2 years. Simple interest: \$_____	6) \$530 at 4% for 5 years. Simple interest: \$_____
Find more at bit.ly/3nJli3D	7) \$5,100 at 6% for 6 months. Simple interest: \$_____	8) \$960 at 5% for 3 months. Simple interest: \$_____

Topic	Simple Interest – Answers
Notes	✓ Simple Interest: The charge for borrowing money or the return for lending it. To solve a simple interest problem, use this formula: Interest = principal x rate x time ⇒ $I = p \times r \times t$
Example	**Find simple interest for $3,000 investment at 5% for 4 years.** **Solution:** Use Interest formula: $I = prt$ ($P = \$3,000$, r = 5% = 0.05 and $t = 4$) Then: $I = 3,000 \times 0.05 \times 4 = \$600$

Your Turn!		
	1) $200 at 3% for 2 years. Simple interest: $12	2) $4,200 at 4% for 5 years. Simple interest: $840
	3) $720 at 2% for 5 years. Simple interest: $72	4) $2,200 at 8% for 4 years. Simple interest: $704
	5) $1,800 at 3% for 2 years. Simple interest: $108	6) $530 at 4% for 5 years. Simple interest: $106
Find more at bit.ly/3nJIi3D 	7) $5,100 at 6% for 6 months. Simple interest: $153	8) $960 at 5% for 3 months. Simple interest: $12

Topic	Simplifying Variable Expressions
Notes	✓ In algebra, a variable is a letter used to stand for a number. The most common letters are: $x, y, z, a, b, c, m, and\ n$. ✓ Algebraic expression is an expression contains integers, variables, and the math operations such as addition, subtraction, multiplication, division, etc. ✓ In an expression, we can combine "like" terms. (values with same variable and same power)
Example	*Simplify this expression.* $(6x + 8x + 9) = ?$ Combine like terms. Then: $(6x + 8x + 9) = 14x + 9$ **(remember you cannot combine variables and numbers).**

Your Turn!	1) $6x + 4 - 7x =$	2) $5 + 3x + 2x =$
	3) $8x + 3 - 3x =$	4) $-2 - x^2 - 6x^2 =$
	5) $3 + 10x^2 + 2 =$	6) $8x^2 + 6x + 7x^2 =$
	7) $5x^2 - 12x^2 + 8x =$	8) $2x^2 - 2x - x + 5x^2 =$
Find more at bit.ly/2WFVudQ	9) $6x - (10 - 25x) =$	10) $16x - (60x - 50) =$

Topic	**Simplifying Variable Expressions – Answers**
Notes	✓ In algebra, a variable is a letter used to stand for a number. The most common letters are: $x, y, z, a, b, c, m, and\ n$. ✓ Algebraic expression is an expression contains integers, variables, and the math operations such as addition, subtraction, multiplication, division, etc. ✓ In an expression, we can combine "like" terms. (values with same variable and same power)
Example	*Simplify this expression*. $(6x + 8x + 9) = ?$ Combine like terms. Then: $(6x + 8x + 9) = 14x + 9$ *(remember you cannot combine variables and numbers).*

Your Turn!		
	1) $6x + 4 - 7x =$ $\quad\quad -x + 4$	2) $5 + 3x + 2x =$ $\quad\quad 5x + 5$
	3) $8x + 3 - 3x =$ $\quad\quad 5x + 3$	4) $-2 - x^2 - 6x^2 =$ $\quad\quad -7x^2 - 2$
	5) $3 + 10x^2 + 2 =$ $\quad\quad 10x^2 + 5$	6) $8x^2 + 6x + 7x^2 =$ $\quad\quad 15x^2 + 6x$
	7) $5x^2 - 12x^2 + 8x =$ $\quad\quad -7x^2 + 8x$	8) $2x^2 - 2x - x + 5x^2 =$ $\quad\quad 7x^2 - 3x$
Find more at bit.ly/2WFVudQ	9) $6x - (10 - 25x) =$ $\quad\quad 31x - 10$	10) $16x - (60x - 50) =$ $\quad\quad -44x + 50$

Topic	Simplifying Polynomial Expressions
Notes	✓ In mathematics, a polynomial is an expression consisting of variables and coefficients that involves only the operations of addition, subtraction, multiplication, and non–negative integer exponents of variables. $P(x) = a_n x^n + a_{n-1} x^{n-1} + \ldots + a_2 x^2 + a_1 x + z$
Example	**Simplify this expression.** $(2x^2 - x^4) - (4x^4 - x^2) =$ First use distributive property: → multiply $(-)$ into $(4x^4 - x^2)$ $(2x^2 - x^4) - (4x^4 - x^2) = 2x^2 - x^4 - 4x^4 + x^2$ Then combine "like" terms: $2x^2 - x^4 - 4x^4 + x^2 = 3x^2 - 5x^4$ And write in standard form: $3x^2 - 5x^4 = -5x^4 + 3x^2$

Your Turn!

1) $(x^3 + 3x^2) - (10x + 4x^2) =$	2) $(3x^5 + 5x^3) - (6x^3 + 9x^2) =$
3) $(12x^4 + 4x^2) - (2x^2 - 6x^4) =$	4) $14x - 3x^2 - 2(6x^2 + 6x^3) =$
5) $(5x^3 - 3) + 5(2x^2 - 3x^3) =$	6) $(4x^3 - 2x) - 2(4x^3 - 2x^4) =$
7) $3(3x - 2x^3) - 4(x^3 + 5x^2) =$	8) $(4x^2 - 3x) - (4x^3 + 6x^2) =$

Find more at

bit.ly/2WT5gtn

Topic	**Simplifying Polynomial Expressions – Answers**
Notes	✓ In mathematics, a polynomial is an expression consisting of variables and coefficients that involves only the operations of addition, subtraction, multiplication, and non–negative integer exponents of variables. $$P(x) = a_n x^n + a_{n-1} x^{n-1} + \ldots + a_2 x^2 + a_1 x + a_0$$
Example	***Simplify this expression.*** $(2x^2 - x^4) - (4x^4 - x^2) =$ First use distributive property: → multiply $(-)$ into $(4x^4 - x^2)$ $(2x^2 - x^4) - (4x^4 - x^2) = 2x^2 - x^4 - 4x^4 + x^2$ Then combine "like" terms: $2x^2 - x^4 - 4x^4 + x^2 = 3x^2 - 5x^4$ And write in standard form: $3x^2 - 5x^4 = -5x^4 + 3x^2$

Your Turn!		
	1) $(x^3 + 3x^2) - (10x + 4x^2) =$ $x^3 - x^2 - 10x$	2) $(3x^5 + 5x^3) - (6x^3 + 9x^2) =$ $3x^5 - x^3 - 9x^2$
	3) $(12x^4 + 4x^2) - (2x^2 - 6x^4) =$ $18x^4 + 2x^2$	4) $14x - 3x^2 - 2(6x^2 + 6x^3) =$ $-12x^3 - 15x^2 + 14x$
	5) $(5x^3 - 3) + 5(2x^2 - 3x^3) =$ $-10x^3 + 10x^2 - 3$	6) $(4x^3 - 2x) - 2(4x^3 - 2x^4) =$ $4x^4 - 4x^3 - 2x$
Find more at bit.ly/2WT5gtn 	7) $3(3x - 2x^3) - 4(x^3 + 5x^2) =$ $-10x^3 - 20x^2 + 9x$	8) $(4x^2 - 3x) - (4x^3 + 6x^2) =$ $-4x^3 - 2x^2 - 3x$

Topic	**Evaluating One Variable**
Notes	✓ To evaluate one variable expression, find the variable and substitute a number for that variable. ✓ Perform the arithmetic operations.
Example	*Find the value of this expression for* $x = -3$. $-3x - 13$ **Solution:** Substitute -3 for x, then: $-3x - 13 = -3(-3) - 13 = 9 - 13 = -4$

Your Turn!		
	1) $x = -2 \Rightarrow 4x + 9 =$ ____	2) $x = 3 \Rightarrow 5(3x + 5) =$ ____
	3) $x = -1 \Rightarrow 6x + 4 =$ ____	4) $x = 7 \Rightarrow 6(5x + 3) =$ ____
	5) $x = 4 \Rightarrow 5(3x + 2) =$ ____	6) $x = 6 \Rightarrow 3(2x + 4) =$ ____
	7) $x = 3 \Rightarrow 7(3x + 1) =$ ____	8) $x = 8 \Rightarrow 3(3x + 7) =$ ____
	9) $x = 8 \Rightarrow 3(x + 6) =$ ____	10) $x = 6 \Rightarrow 3(2x + 3) =$ ____

Find more at

bit.ly/3ppujQZ

Topic	**Evaluating One Variable – Answers**
Notes	✓ To evaluate one variable expression, find the variable and substitute a number for that variable. ✓ Perform the arithmetic operations.
Example	*Find the value of this expression for* $x = -3$. $-3x - 13$ **Solution:** Substitute -3 for x, then: $-3x - 13 = -3(-3) - 13 = 9 - 13 = -4$

Your Turn!		
	1) $x = -2 \Rightarrow 4x + 9 = 1$	2) $x = 3 \Rightarrow 5(3x + 5) = 70$
	3) $x = -1 \Rightarrow 6x + 4 = -2$	4) $x = 7 \Rightarrow 6(5x + 3) = 228$
	5) $x = 4 \Rightarrow 5(3x + 2) = 70$	6) $x = 6 \Rightarrow 3(2x + 4) = 48$
	7) $x = 3 \Rightarrow 7(3x + 1) = 70$	8) $x = 8 \Rightarrow 3(3x + 7) = 93$
Find more at bit.ly/3ppujQZ	9) $x = 8 \Rightarrow 3(x + 6) = 42$	10) $x = 6 \Rightarrow 3(2x + 3) = 45$

Topic	**Evaluating Two Variables**
Notes	✓ To evaluate an algebraic expression, substitute a number for each variable. ✓ Perform the arithmetic operations to find the value of the expression.
Example	***Evaluate this expression for*** $a = 4$ ***and*** $b = -2$. $5a - 6b$ **Solution:** Substitute 4 for a, and -2 for b, then: $$5a - 6b = 5(4) - 6(-2) = 20 + 12 = 32$$

Your Turn!		
	1) $-3a + 5b$, $a = 3$, $b = 2$ ————	2) $4x + 2y$, $x = -1$, $y = 4$ ————
	3) $-5a + 3b$, $a = 2$, $b = -2$ ————	4) $3x - 4y$, $x = 6$, $y = 2$ ————
	5) $2z + 14 + 6k$, $z = 5$, $k = 3$ ————	6) $7a - (9 - 3b)$, $a = 1$, $b = 1$ ————
	7) $-6a + 3b$, $a = 4$, $b = 3$ ————	8) $-2a + b$, $a = 6$, $b = 9$ ————
	9) $5x + 3y$, $x = 2$, $y = 9$ ————	10) $z + 7 + 3k$, $z = 4$, $k = 2$ ————

Find more at

bit.ly/2JfrzWJ

Topic	**Evaluating Two Variables – Answers**
Notes	✓ To evaluate an algebraic expression, substitute a number for each variable. ✓ Perform the arithmetic operations to find the value of the expression.
Example	**Evaluate this expression for** $a = 4$ **and** $b = -2$. $5a - 6b$ **Solution:** Substitute 4 for a, and -2 for b, then: $5a - 6b = 5(4) - 6(-2) = 20 + 12 = 32$

Your Turn!	1) $-3a + 5b,\ a = 3,\ b = 2$ 1	2) $4x + 2y,\ x = -1,\ y = 4$ 4
	3) $-5a + 3b,\ a = 2,\ b = -2$ -16	4) $3x - 4y,\ x = 6,\ y = 2$ 10
	5) $2z + 14 + 6k,\ z = 5,\ k = 3$ 42	6) $7a - (9 - 3b),\ a = 1,\ b = 1$ 1
	7) $-6a + 3b,\ a = 4,\ b = 3$ -15	8) $-2a + b,\ a = 6,\ b = 9$ -3
Find more at bit.ly/2JfrzWJ	9) $5x + 3y,\ x = 2,\ y = 9$ 37	10) $z + 7 + 3k,\ z = 4,\ k = 2$ 17

Topic	The Distributive Property
Notes	✓ The distributive property (or the distributive property of multiplication over addition and subtraction) simplifies and solves expressions in the form of: $a(b + c)$ or $a(b - c)$ ✓ Distributive Property rule: $$a(b + c) = ab + ac$$
Example	***Simply.*** $(5)(2x - 8)$ **Solution:** Use Distributive Property rule: $a(b + c) = ab + ac$ $$(5)(2x - 8) = (5 \times 2x) + (5) \times (-8) = 10x - 40$$

Your Turn!		
	1) $(-3)(2 - 4x) =$	2) $(3 - 2x)(-5)$
	3) $6\,(5 - 9x) =$	4) $10(3 - 5x) =$
	5) $5(6 - 5x) =$	6) $(-2)(-5x + 3) =$
	7) $(8 - 9x)(5) =$	8) $(-16x + 15)(-3) =$
Find more at bit.ly/38qCaXs	9) $(-6x + 8)(4) =$	10) $(-12x + 21)(-3) =$

Topic	The Distributive Property – Answers
Notes	✓ The distributive property (or the distributive property of multiplication over addition and subtraction) simplifies and solves expressions in the form of: $a(b + c)$ or $a(b - c)$ ✓ Distributive Property rule: $$a(b + c) = ab + ac$$
Example	***Simply.*** $(5)(2x - 8)$ **Solution:** Use Distributive Property rule: $a(b + c) = ab + ac$ $$(5)(2x - 8) = (5 \times 2x) + (5) \times (-8) = 10x - 40$$

Your Turn!		
	1) $(-3)(2 - 4x) = 12x - 6$	2) $(3 - 2x)(-5) = 10x - 15$
	3) $6(5 - 9x) = -54x + 30$	4) $10(3 - 5x) = -50x + 30$
	5) $5(6 - 5x) = -25x + 30$	6) $(-2)(-5x + 3) = 10x - 6$
	7) $(8 - 9x)(5) = -45x + 40$	8) $(-16x + 15)(-3) =$ $48x - 45$
	9) $(-6x + 8)(4) = -24x + 32$	10) $(-12x + 21)(-3) =$ $36x - 63$

Find more at

bit.ly/38qCaXs

Topic	One–Step Equations

Notes	✓ You only need to perform one Math operation in order to solve the one-step equations.
	
	✓ To solve one-step equation, find the inverse (opposite) operation is being performed.
	
	✓ The inverse operations are:
	
	   - Addition and subtraction
	
	   - Multiplication and division

Example	***Solve this equation.*** $x + 42 = 60 \Rightarrow x = ?$ Here, the operation is addition and its inverse operation is subtraction. To solve this equation, subtract 42 from both sides of the *equation:* $x + 42 - 42 = 60 - 42$ Then simplify: $x + 42 - 42 = 60 - 42 \Rightarrow x = 18$

Your Turn!	1) $x - 12 = 44 \Rightarrow x = $ ____	2) $15 = 11 + x \Rightarrow x = $ ____
	3) $x - 22 = 54 \Rightarrow x = $ ___	4) $x + 14 = 24 \Rightarrow x = $ ___
	5) $4x = 24 \Rightarrow x = $ ___	6) $\frac{x}{6} = -3 \Rightarrow x = $ ___
Find more at bit.ly/37Jq0tK	7) $66 = 22x \Rightarrow x = $ ___	8) $\frac{x}{18} = 3 \Rightarrow x = $ ___

Topic	One–Step Equations – Answers

Notes	✓ You only need to perform one Math operation in order to solve the one-step equations.
	 ✓ To solve one-step equation, find the inverse (opposite) operation is being performed.
	 ✓ The inverse operations are:
	    - Addition and subtraction
	    - Multiplication and division

Example	*Solve this equation.* $x + 42 = 60 \Rightarrow x = ?$ Here, the operation is addition and its inverse operation is subtraction. To solve this equation, subtract 42 from both sides of the *equation:* $x + 42 - 42 = 60 - 42$ Then simplify: $x + 42 - 42 = 60 - 42 \Rightarrow x = 18$

Your Turn! **Find more at** bit.ly/37Jq0tK	1) $x - 12 = 44 \Rightarrow x = 56$	2) $15 = 11 + x \Rightarrow x = 4$
	3) $x - 22 = 54 \Rightarrow x = 76$	4) $x + 14 = 24 \Rightarrow x = 10$
	5) $4x = 24 \Rightarrow x = 6$	6) $\frac{x}{6} = -3 \Rightarrow x = -18$
	7) $66 = 22x \Rightarrow x = 3$	8) $\frac{x}{18} = 3 \Rightarrow x = 54$

Topic	**Multi –Step Equations**
Notes	✓ Combine "like" terms on one side. ✓ Bring variables to one side by adding or subtracting. ✓ Simplify using the inverse of addition or subtraction. ✓ Simplify further by using the inverse of multiplication or division. ✓ Check your solution by plugging the value of the variable into the original equation.
Example	*Solve this equation for* x. $\quad 2x - 3 = 13$ **Solution:** The inverse of subtraction is addition. Add 3 to both sides of the equation. Then: $2x - 3 = 13 \Rightarrow 2x - 3 = 13 + 3$ $\Rightarrow 2x = 16$. Now, divide both sides by 2, then: $\frac{2x}{2} = \frac{16}{2} \Rightarrow x = 8$ Now, check the solution: $x = 8 \Rightarrow 2x - 3 = 13 \Rightarrow 2(8) - 3 = 13 \Rightarrow 16 - 3 = 13 \qquad$ The answer $x = 8$ is correct.

Your Turn!	1) $5x - 15 = 10 \Rightarrow x =$	2) $14 - 2x = -6 + 2x \Rightarrow x =$
	3) $3(4 - 2x) = 24 \Rightarrow x =$	4) $15 + 5x = -7 - 6x \Rightarrow x =$
	5) $-2(5 + x) = 2 \Rightarrow x =$	6) $12 - 2x = -3 - 5x \Rightarrow x =$
Find more at bit.ly/3nQbSEB	7) $18 = -(x - 8) \Rightarrow x =$	8) $13 - 5x = -5 - 2x \Rightarrow x =$

Topic	Multi –Step Equations – Answers
Notes	✓ Combine "like" terms on one side. ✓ Bring variables to one side by adding or subtracting. ✓ Simplify using the inverse of addition or subtraction. ✓ Simplify further by using the inverse of multiplication or division. ✓ Check your solution by plugging the value of the variable into the original equation.
Example	***Solve this equation for*** x. $2x - 3 = 13$ **Solution:** The inverse of subtraction is addition. Add 3 to both sides of the equation. Then: $2x - 3 = 13 \Rightarrow 2x - 3 = 13 + 3$ $\Rightarrow 2x = 16$. Now, divide both sides by 2, then: $\frac{2x}{2} = \frac{16}{2} \Rightarrow x = 8$ Now, check the solution: $x = 8 \Rightarrow 2x - 3 = 13 \Rightarrow 2(8) - 3 = 13 \Rightarrow 16 - 3 = 13$ The answer $x = 8$ is correct.

Your Turn!	1) $5x - 15 = 10 \Rightarrow x = 5$	2) $14 - 2x = -6 + 2x \Rightarrow x = 5$
	3) $3(4 - 2x) = 24 \Rightarrow x = -2$	4) $15 + 5x = -7 - 6x \Rightarrow x = -2$
Find more at bit.ly/3nObSFB	5) $-2(5 + x) = 2 \Rightarrow x = -6$	6) $12 - 2x = -3 - 5x \Rightarrow x = -5$
	7) $18 = -(x - 8) \Rightarrow x = -10$	8) $13 - 5x = -5 - 2x \Rightarrow x = 6$

Topic	System of Equations
Notes	✓ A system of equations contains two equations and two variables. For example, consider the system of equations: $x - 2y = -2, x + 2y = 10$ ✓ The easiest way to solve a system of equation is using the elimination method. The elimination method uses the addition property of equality. You can add the same value to each side of an equation. ✓ For the first equation above, you can add $x + 2y$ to the left side and 10 to the right side of the first equation: $x - 2y + (x + 2y) = -2 + 10$. Now, if you simplify, you get: $x - 2y + (x + 2y) = -2 + 10 \rightarrow 2x = 8 \rightarrow x = 4$. Now, substitute 4 for the x in the first equation: $4 - 2y = -2$. By solving this equation, $y = 3$
Example	What is the value of x and y in this system of equations? $\begin{cases} 3x - y = 7 \\ -x + 4y = 5 \end{cases}$ **Solution:** Solving System of Equations by Elimination: $\begin{array}{l} 3x - y = 7 \\ \underline{-x + 4y = 5} \end{array}$ Multiply the second equation by 3, then add it to the first equation. $\begin{array}{l} 3x - y = 7 \\ \underline{3(-x + 4y = 5)} \end{array} \Rightarrow \begin{array}{l} 3x - y = 7 \\ \underline{-3x + 12y = 15} \end{array} \Rightarrow 11y = 22 \Rightarrow y = 2.$ Now, substitute 2 for y in the first equation and solve for x. $3x - (2) = 7 \Rightarrow 3x = 9 \Rightarrow x = 3$
Your Turn! **Find more at** bit.ly/3mPGO6k	1) $-4x + 4y = 8$ $\qquad -4x + 2y = 6$ $x = $ ___ $y = $ ___ 2) $-5x + y = -3$ $\qquad 3x - 8y = 24$ $x = $ ___ $y = $ ___ 3) $y = -2$ $\qquad 4x - 3y = 8$ $x = $ ___ $y = $ ___ 4) $y = -3x + 5$ $\qquad 5x - 4y = -3$ $x = $ ___ $y = $ ___ 5) $20x - 18y = -26$ $\qquad -10x + 6y = 22$ $x = $ ___ $y = $ ___ 6) $-9x - 12y = 15$ $\qquad 2x - 6y = 14$ $x = $ ___ $\qquad y = $ ___

Topic	System of Equations- Answers
Notes	✓ A system of equations contains two equations and two variables. For example, consider the system of equations: $x - 2y = -2, x + 2y = 10$ ✓ The easiest way to solve a system of equation is using the elimination method. The elimination method uses the addition property of equality. You can add the same value to each side of an equation. ✓ For the first equation above, you can add $x + 2y$ to the left side and 10 to the right side of the first equation: $x - 2y + (x + 2y) = -2 + 10$. Now, if you simplify, you get: $x - 2y + (x + 2y) = -2 + 10 \rightarrow 2x = 8 \rightarrow x = 4$. Now, substitute 4 for the x in the first equation: $4 - 2y = -2$. By solving this equation, $y = 3$
Example	What is the value of x and y in this system of equations? $\begin{cases} 3x - y = 7 \\ -x + 4y = 5 \end{cases}$ **Solution:** Solving System of Equations by Elimination: $\begin{array}{l} 3x - y = 7 \\ \underline{-x + 4y = 5} \end{array}$ Multiply the second equation by 3, then add it to the first equation. $\begin{array}{l} 3x - y = 7 \\ \underline{3(-x + 4y = 5)} \end{array} \Rightarrow \begin{array}{l} 3x - y = 7 \\ \underline{-3x + 12y = 15} \end{array} \Rightarrow 11y = 22 \Rightarrow y = 2.$ Now, substitute 2 for y in the first equation and solve for x. $3x - (2) = 7 \Rightarrow 3x = 9 \Rightarrow x = 3$
Your Turn! **Find more at** bit.ly/3mPGO6k 	1) $-4x + 4y = 8$ $-4x + 2y = 6$ $x = -1$ $y = 1$ 2) $-5x + y = -3$ $3x - 8y = 24$ $x = 0$ $y = -3$ 3) $y = -2$ $4x - 3y = 8$ $x = \dfrac{1}{2}$ $y = -2$ 4) $y = -3x + 5$ $5x - 4y = -3$ $x = 1$ $y = 2$ 5) $20x - 18y = -26$ $-10x + 6y = 22$ $x = -4$ $y = -3$ 6) $-9x - 12y = 15$ $2x - 6y = 14$ $x = 1$ $y = -2$

Topic	**Graphing Single–Variable Inequalities**
Notes	✓ An inequality compares two expressions using an inequality sign. ✓ Inequality signs are: "less than" <, "greater than" >, "less than or equal to" ≤, and "greater than or equal to" ≥. ✓ To graph a single–variable inequality, find the value of the inequality on the number line. ✓ For less than (<) or greater than (>) draw open circle on the value of the variable. If there is an equal sign too, then use filled circle. ✓ Draw an arrow to the right for greater or to the left for less than.
Example	***Draw a graph for this inequality.*** $x < 5$ **Solution:** Since, the variable is less than 5, then we need to find 5 in the number line and draw an open circle on it. Then, draw an arrow to the left.

Your Turn!	1) $x < 3$	2) $x \geq -2$
	3) $x \geq -3$	4) $x \leq 6$
Find more at bit.ly/3aJ4GGo 	5) $x > -6$	6) $2 > x$
	7) $-3 \leq x$	8) $x > 1$

Topic	Graphing Single–Variable Inequalities- Answers
Notes	✓ An inequality compares two expressions using an inequality sign. ✓ Inequality signs are: "less than" $<$, "greater than" $>$, "less than or equal to" $\leq$, and "greater than or equal to" $\geq$. ✓ To graph a single–variable inequality, find the value of the inequality on the number line. ✓ For less than ($<$) or greater than ($>$) draw open circle on the value of the variable. If there is an equal sign too, then use filled circle. ✓ Draw an arrow to the right for greater or to the left for less than.
Example	**Draw a graph for this inequality.** $x < 5$ **Solution:** Since, the variable is less than 5, then we need to find 5 in the number line and draw an open circle on it. Then, draw an arrow to the left.

Your Turn!
 	
Find more at
bit.ly/3aJ4GGo
 	
	1) $x < 3$
	    2) $x \geq -2$
	
	3) $x \geq -3$
	    4) $x \leq 6$
	
	5) $x > -6$
	    6) $2 > x$
	
	7) $-3 \leq x$
	    8) $x > 1$

Topic	One–Step Inequalities
Notes	✓ Inequality signs are: "less than" $<$, "greater than" $>$, "less than or equal to" $\leq$, and "greater than or equal to" $\geq$. ✓ You only need to perform one Math operation in order to solve the one-step inequalities. ✓ To solve one-step inequalities, find the inverse (opposite) operation is being performed. ✓ For dividing or multiplying both sides by negative numbers, flip the direction of the inequality sign.
Example	***Solve this inequality.*** $x + 12 < 60 \Rightarrow$ _____ Here, the operation is addition and its inverse operation is subtraction. To solve this inequality, subtract 12 from both sides of the ***inequality:*** $x + 12 - 12 < 60 - 12$ Then simplify: $x < 48$

Your Turn!	1) $3x < -9 \Rightarrow$ _____	2) $x + 5 > 29 \Rightarrow$ _____
	3) $-3x \geq 36 \Rightarrow$ _____	4) $x - 16 \leq 4 \Rightarrow$ _____
	5) $\frac{x}{2} \geq -9 \Rightarrow$ _____	6) $48 < 6x \Rightarrow$ _____
Find more at bit.ly/3rrElgL	7) $88 \leq 22x \Rightarrow$ _____	8) $\frac{x}{6} > 8 \Rightarrow$ _____

Topic	One–Step Inequalities - Answers
Notes	✓ Inequality signs are: "less than" $<$, "greater than" $>$, "less than or equal to" $\leq$, and "greater than or equal to" $\geq$. ✓ You only need to perform one Math operation in order to solve the one-step inequalities. ✓ To solve one-step inequalities, find the inverse (opposite) operation is being performed. ✓ For dividing or multiplying both sides by negative numbers, flip the direction of the inequality sign.
Example	*Solve this inequality.* $x + 12 < 60 \Rightarrow$ _____ Here, the operation is addition and its inverse operation is subtraction. To solve this inequality, subtract 12 from both sides of the *inequality:* $x + 12 - 12 < 60 - 12$ Then simplify: $x < 48$

Your Turn!		
	1) $3x < -9 \Rightarrow x < -3$	2) $x + 5 > 29 \Rightarrow x > 24$
	3) $-3x \geq 36 \Rightarrow x \leq -12$	4) $x - 16 \leq 4 \Rightarrow x \leq 20$
Find more at bit.ly/3rrElgL	5) $\frac{x}{2} \geq -9 \Rightarrow x \geq -18$	6) $48 < 6x \Rightarrow 8 < x$
	7) $88 \leq 22x \Rightarrow 4 \leq x$	8) $\frac{x}{6} > 8 \Rightarrow x > 48$

Topic	Multi –Step Inequalities
Notes	✓ Isolate the variable. ✓ Simplify using the inverse of addition or subtraction. ✓ Simplify further by using the inverse of multiplication or division. ✓ For dividing or multiplying both sides by negative numbers, flip the direction of the inequality sign.
Example	*Solve this inequality*. $3x + 12 \leq 21$ **Solution:** First subtract 12 from both sides: $3x + 12 - 12 \leq 21 - 12$ Then simplify: $3x + 12 - 12 \leq 21 - 12 \rightarrow 3x \leq 9$ Now divide both sides by 3: $\frac{3x}{3} \leq \frac{9}{3} \rightarrow x \leq 3$
Your Turn! **Find more at** bit.ly/2WK1xOr	1) $4x + 3 < 39 \rightarrow$ _____ 2) $5x - 9 \leq 6 \rightarrow$ _____ 3) $2x - 5 \leq 17 \rightarrow$ _____ 4) $14 - 7x \geq -7 \rightarrow$ _____ 5) $18 - 6x \geq -6 \rightarrow$ _____ 6) $2x - 18 \leq 16 \rightarrow$ _____ 7) $9 + 6x < 45 \rightarrow$ _____ 8) $7 - 4x < 19 \rightarrow$ _____

Topic	Multi –Step Inequalities – Answers
Notes	✓ Isolate the variable. ✓ Simplify using the inverse of addition or subtraction. ✓ Simplify further by using the inverse of multiplication or division. ✓ For dividing or multiplying both sides by negative numbers, flip the direction of the inequality sign.
Example	*Solve this inequality*. $3x + 12 \leq 21$ **Solution:** First subtract 12 from both sides: $3x + 12 - 12 \leq 21 - 12$ Then simplify: $3x + 12 - 12 \leq 21 - 12 \rightarrow 3x \leq 9$ Now divide both sides by 3: $\frac{3x}{3} \leq \frac{9}{3} \rightarrow x \leq 3$

Your Turn!		
	1) $4x + 3 < 39 \rightarrow x < 9$	2) $5x - 9 \leq 6 \rightarrow x \leq 3$
	3) $2x - 5 \leq 17 \rightarrow x \leq 11$	4) $14 - 7x \geq -7 \rightarrow x \leq 3$
	5) $18 - 6x \geq -6 \rightarrow x \leq 4$	6) $2x - 18 \leq 16 \rightarrow x \leq 17$
Find more at bit.ly/2WK1xOr	7) $9 + 6x < 45 \rightarrow x < 6$	8) $7 - 4x < 19 \rightarrow x > -3$

Topic	**Finding Slope**
Notes	✓ The slope of a line represents the direction of a line on the coordinate plane. ✓ A line on coordinate plane can be drawn by connecting two points. ✓ To find the slope of a line, we need two points. ✓ The slope of a line with two points A (x_1, y_1) and B (x_2, y_2) can be found by using this formula: $\frac{y_2 - y_1}{x_2 - x_1} = \frac{rise}{run}$ ✓ The equation of a line is typically written as $y = mx + b$ where m is the slope and b is the y-intercept.
Examples	*Find the slope of the line through these two points:* $(4, -12)$ *and* $(9, 8)$. **Solution:** Slope $= \frac{y_2 - y_1}{x_2 - x_1}$. Let (x_1, y_1) be $(4, -12)$ and (x_2, y_2) be $(9, 8)$. **Then:** slope $= \frac{y_2 - y_1}{x_2 - x_1} = \frac{8 - (-12)}{9 - 4} = \frac{8 + 12}{5} = \frac{20}{5} = 4$ *Find the slope of the line with equation* $y = 5x - 6$ **Solution:** when the equation of a line is written in the form of $y = mx + b$, the slope is m. In this line: $y = 5x - 6$, the slope is 5.

Your Turn!	1) $(1, 3), (5, 7)$ Slope = ____	2) $(-2, 2), (0, 4)$ Slope = ____
	3) $(4, -2), (2, 4)$ Slope = ____	4) $(-4, -1), (0, 7)$ Slope = ____
Find more at bit.ly/3nMJYJv	5) $y = 4x + 15$ Slope = ____	6) $y = -6x + 3$ Slope = ____

Topic	Finding Slope – Answers
Notes	✓ The slope of a line represents the direction of a line on the coordinate plane. ✓ A line on coordinate plane can be drawn by connecting two points. ✓ To find the slope of a line, we need two points. ✓ The slope of a line with two points A (x_1, y_1) and B (x_2, y_2) can be found by using this formula: $\frac{y_2 - y_1}{x_2 - x_1} = \frac{rise}{run}$ ✓ The equation of a line is typically written as $y = mx + b$ where m is the slope and b is the y-intercept.
Examples	**Find the slope of the line through these two points:** $(4, -12) \ and \ (9, 8)$. **Solution:** Slope $= \frac{y_2 - y_1}{x_2 - x_1}$. Let (x_1, y_1) be $(4, -12)$ and (x_2, y_2) be $(9, 8)$. **Then:** slope $= \frac{y_2 - y_1}{x_2 - x_1} = \frac{8 - (-12)}{9 - 4} = \frac{8 + 12}{5} = \frac{20}{5} = 4$ **Find the slope of the line with equation** $y = 5x - 6$ **Solution:** when the equation of a line is written in the form of $y = mx + b$, the slope is m. In this line: $y = 5x - 6$, the slope is 5.
Your Turn!	1) $(1, 3), (5, 7)$ 2) $(-2, 2), (0, 4)$ Slope $= 1$ Slope $= 1$
	3) $(4, -2), (2, 4)$ 4) $(-4, -1), (0, 7)$ Slope $= -3$ Slope $= 2$
Find more at bit.ly/3nMJYJv 	5) $y = 4x + 15$ 6) $y = 6x + 3$ Slope $= 4$ Slope $= 6$

Topic	**Graphing Lines Using Slope–Intercept Form**
Notes	✓ Slope–intercept form of a line: given the slope m and the y–intercept (the intersection of the line and y-axis) b, then the equation of the line is: $$y = mx + b$$
Example	***Sketch the graph of*** $y = -2\text{x} - 1$. **Solution:** To graph this line, we need to find two points. When x is zero the value of y is -1. And when y is zero the value of x is $-\frac{1}{2}$. $$x = 0 \rightarrow y = -2(0) - 1 = -1, y = 0 \rightarrow 0$$ $$= -2x - 1 \rightarrow x = -\frac{1}{2}$$ Now, we have two points: $(0, -1)$ and $(-\frac{1}{2}, 0)$. Find the points and graph the line. Remember that the slope of the line is $-\frac{1}{2}$.
Your Turn! **Find more at** bit.ly/3hfdnJL	1) $y = -4x + 1$　　　　2) $y = -x - 5$

Topic	Graphing Lines Using Slope–Intercept Form - Answers
Notes	✓ Slope–intercept form of a line: given the slope m and the y–intercept (the intersection of the line and y-axis) b, then the equation of the line is: $$y = mx + b$$
Example	**Sketch the graph of** $y = -2x - 1$. **Solution:** To graph this line, we need to find two points. When x is zero the value of y is -1. And when y is zero the value of x is $-\frac{1}{2}$. $$x = 0 \to y = -2(0) - 1 = -1, y = 0 \to 0$$ $$= -2x - 1 \to x = -\frac{1}{2}$$ Now, we have two points: $(0, -1)$ and $(-\frac{1}{2}, 0)$. Find the points and graph the line. Remember that the slope of the line is $-\frac{1}{2}$.
Your Turn! **Find more at** bit.ly/3hfdnJL 	1) $y = -4x + 1$ 2) $y = -x - 5$

Topic	**Writing Linear Equations**	
Notes	✓ The equation of a line: $y = mx + b$ ✓ Identify the slope. ✓ Find the y–intercept. This can be done by substituting the slope and the coordinates of a point (x, y) on the line.	
Example	**Write the equation of the line through $(3, 1)$ and $(-1, 5)$.** **Solution:** $Slop = \frac{y_2 - y_1}{x_2 - x_1} = \frac{5-1}{-1-3} = \frac{4}{-4} = -1 \rightarrow m = -1$ To find the value of b, you can use either points. The answer will be the same: $y = -x + b$ $(3, 1) \rightarrow 1 = -3 + b \rightarrow b = 4$ $(-1, 5) \rightarrow 5 = -(-1) + b \rightarrow b = 4$ The equation of the line is: $y = -x + 4$	
Your Turn!	1) through: $(-1, 2), (1, 4)$ $y =$	2) through: $(8, 1), (5, 4)$ $y =$
	3) through: $(5, -1), (8, 2)$ $y =$	4) through: $(-2, 4), (4, -8)$ $y =$
Find more at bit.ly/3nMKcAl	5) through: $(6, -5), (-5, 6)$ $y =$	6) through: $(4, -4), (-2, 8)$ $y =$
	7) through $(-3, 6)$, Slope: 2 $y =$	8) through $(4, 3)$, Slope: -4 $y =$

Topic	Writing Linear Equations – Answers
Notes	✓ The equation of a line: $y = mx + b$ ✓ Identify the slope. ✓ Find the y–intercept. This can be done by substituting the slope and the coordinates of a point (x, y) on the line.
Example	**Write the equation of the line through $(3, 1)$ and $(-1, 5)$.** **Solution:** $Slop = \frac{y_2 - y_1}{x_2 - x_1} = \frac{5 - 1}{-1 - 3} = \frac{4}{-4} = -1 \rightarrow m = -1$ To find the value of b, you can use either points. The answer will be the same: $y = -x + b$ $(3, 1) \rightarrow 1 = -3 + b \rightarrow b = 4$ $(-1, 5) \rightarrow 5 = -(-1) + b \rightarrow b = 4$ The equation of the line is: $y = -x + 4$

Your Turn!

1) through: $(-1, 2), (1, 4)$ $y = x + 3$	2) through: $(8, 1), (5, 4)$ $y = -x + 9$
3) through: $(5, -1), (8, 2)$ $y = x - 6$	4) through: $(-2, 4), (4, -8)$ $y = -2x$
5) through: $(6, -5), (-5, 6)$ $y = -x + 1$	6) through: $(4, -4), (-2, 8)$ $y = -2x + 4$
7) through $(-3, 6)$, Slope: 2 $y = 2x + 12$	8) through $(4, 3)$, Slope: -4 $y = -4x + 19$

Find more at

bit.ly/3nMKcAl

Topic	**Finding Midpoint**
Notes	✓ The middle of a line segment is its midpoint. ✓ The Midpoint of two endpoints A (x_1, y_1) and B (x_2, y_2) can be found using this formula: $M(\frac{x_1+x_2}{2}, \frac{y_1+y_2}{2})$
Example	Find the midpoint of the line segment with the given endpoints. $(1, -2), (3, 6)$ **Solution:** Midpoint $= (\frac{x_1+x_2}{2}, \frac{y_1+y_2}{2}) \rightarrow (x_1, y_1) = (1, -2)$ and $(x_2, y_2) = (3, 6)$ Midpoint $= (\frac{1+3}{2}, \frac{-2+6}{2}) \rightarrow (\frac{4}{2}, \frac{4}{2}) \rightarrow M(2, 2)$

Your Turn!	1) $(2, 1), (-4, 1)$ *Midpoint* $= (\_\_, \_\_)$	2) $(6, -2), (2, 4)$ *Midpoint* $= (\_\_, \_\_)$
	3) $(-3, 4), (-5, 0)$ *Midpoint* $= (\_\_, \_\_)$	4) $(8, 1), (-4, 5)$ *Midpoint* $= (\_\_, \_\_)$
	5) $(6, 7), (-4, 5)$ *Midpoint* $= (\_\_, \_\_)$	6) $(2, -3), (2, 5)$ *Midpoint* $= (\_\_, \_\_)$
Find more at bit.ly/3nPdnTg	7) $(7, 3), (-1, -7)$ *Midpoint* $= (\_\_, \_\_)$	8) $(3, 9), (-1, 5)$ *Midpoint* $= (\_\_, \_\_)$
	9) $(5, 2), (-9, 0)$ *Midpoint* $= (\_\_, \_\_)$	10) $(2, 7), (10, -9)$ *Midpoint* $= (\_\_, \_\_)$

Topic	Finding Midpoint – Answers
Notes	✓ The middle of a line segment is its midpoint. ✓ The Midpoint of two endpoints A (x_1, y_1) and B (x_2, y_2) can be found using this formula: $M(\frac{x_1+x_2}{2}, \frac{y_1+y_2}{2})$
Example	Find the midpoint of the line segment with the given endpoints. $(\mathbf{1}, -\mathbf{2}), (\mathbf{3}, \mathbf{6})$ **Solution:** Midpoint $= (\frac{x_1+x_2}{2}, \frac{y_1+y_2}{2}) \rightarrow (x_1, y_1) = (1, -2)$ and $(x_2, y_2) = (3, 6)$ Midpoint $= (\frac{1+3}{2}, \frac{-2+6}{2}) \rightarrow (\frac{4}{2}, \frac{4}{2}) \rightarrow M(2, 2)$

Your Turn!	1) $(2, 1), (-4, 1)$ **Midpoint** $= (-1, 1)$	2) $(6, -2), (2, 4)$ **Midpoint** $= (4, 1)$
	3) $(-3, 4), (-5, 0)$ **Midpoint** $= (-4, 2)$	4) $(8, 1), (-4, 5)$ **Midpoint** $= (2, 3)$
	5) $(6, 7), (-4, 5)$ **Midpoint** $= (1, 6)$	6) $(2, -3), (2, 5)$ **Midpoint** $= (2, 1)$
	7) $(7, 3), (-1, -7)$ **Midpoint** $= (3, -2)$	8) $(3, 9), (-1, 5)$ **Midpoint** $= (1, 7)$
Find more at bit.ly/3nPdnTq	9) $(5, 2), (-9, 0)$ **Midpoint** $= (-2, 1)$	10) $(2, 7), (10, -9)$ **Midpoint** $= (6, -1)$

Topic	**Finding Distance of Two Points**
Notes	✓ Use this formula to find the distance of two points A (x_1, y_1) and B (x_2, y_2): $$d = \sqrt{(x_2 - x_1)^2 + (y_2 - y_1)^2}$$
Example	*Find the distance of two points* $(-1, 5)$ and $(4, -7)$. **Solution:** *Use distance of two points formula:* $d = \sqrt{(x_2 - x_1)^2 + (y_2 - y_1)^2}$ $(x_1, y_1) = (-1, 5)$, and $(x_2, y_2) = (4, -7)$ Then: $d = \sqrt{(x_2 - x_1)^2 + (y_2 - y_1)^2} \to d =$ $\sqrt{(4 - (-1))^2 + (-7 - 5)^2} = \sqrt{(5)^2 + (-12)^2} = \sqrt{25 + 144} =$ $\sqrt{169} = 13$

Your Turn!

1) $(8, 2), (-6, 2)$ Distance = ____   2) $(3, -4), (3, 6)$ Distance = ____

3) $(-5, 10), (7, 1)$ Distance = ____   4) $(8, 1), (-4, 6)$ Distance = ____

5) $(-3, 6), (-4, 5)$ Distance = ____   6) $(4, -1), (14, 23)$ Distance = ____

7) $(3, 5), (6, 9)$ Distance = ____   8) $(2, -2), (10, 4)$ Distance = ____

Find more at
bit.ly/2KV50Hy

Topic	Finding Distance of Two Points - Answers
Notes	✓ Use this formula to find the distance of two points A (x_1, y_1) and B (x_2, y_2): $$d = \sqrt{(x_2 - x_1)^2 + (y_2 - y_1)^2}$$
Example	*Find the distance of two points* $(-1, 5)$ and $(4, -7)$. **Solution:** *Use distance of two points formula:* $d = \sqrt{(x_2 - x_1)^2 + (y_2 - y_1)^2}$ $(x_1, y_1) = (-1, 5)$, and $(x_2, y_2) = (4, -7)$ Then: $d = \sqrt{(x_2 - x_1)^2 + (y_2 - y_1)^2} \rightarrow d = \sqrt{(4 - (-1))^2 + (-7 - 5)^2} = \sqrt{(5)^2 + (-12)^2} = \sqrt{25 + 144} = \sqrt{169} = 13$

Your Turn!		
	1) $(8, 2), (-6, 2)$ **Distance** $= 14$	2) $(3, -4), (3, 6)$ **Distance** $= 10$
	3) $(-5, 10), (7, 1)$ **Distance** $= 15$	4) $(8, 1), (-4, 6)$ **Distance** $= 13$
	5) $(-3, 6), (-4, 5)$ **Distance** $= \sqrt{2}$	6) $(4, -1), (14, 23)$ **Distance** $= 26$
Find more at bit.ly/2KV50Hy	7) $(3, 5), (6, 9)$ **Distance** $= 5$	8) $(2, -2), (10, 4)$ **Distance** $= 10$

Topic	**Multiplication Property of Exponents**
Notes	✓ Exponents are shorthand for repeated multiplication of the same number by itself. For example, instead of 2×2, we can write 2^2. For $3 \times 3 \times 3 \times 3$, we can write 3^4 ✓ In algebra, a variable is a letter used to stand for a number. The most common letters are: $x, y, z, a, b, c, m,$ and n. ✓ Exponent's rules: $x^a \times x^b = x^{a+b}$, $\dfrac{x^a}{x^b} = x^{a-b}$ $(x^a)^b = x^{a \times b}$ $\qquad$ $(xy)^a = x^a \times y^a$ $\qquad$ $\left(\dfrac{a}{b}\right)^c = \dfrac{a^c}{b^c}$
Example	*Multiply.* $4x^3 \times 2x^2$ Use Exponent's rules: $x^a \times x^b = x^{a+b} \rightarrow x^3 \times x^2 = x^{3+2} = x^5$ Then: $4x^3 \times 2x^2 = 8x^5$
Your Turn!	

1) $x^2 \times 5x =$	2) $3x^4 \times x^2 =$
3) $3x^2 \times 4x^5 =$	4) $3x^2 \times 6xy =$
5) $3x^5y \times 5x^2y^3 =$	6) $3x^2y^2 \times 5x^2y^8 =$
7) $5x^2y \times 5x^2y^7 =$	8) $6x^6 \times 4x^9y^4 =$
9) $4x^2y^5 \times 6x^5y^3 =$	10) $10x^6x^2 \times 7xy^5 =$

Find more at

bit.ly/34AWHr1

Topic	**Multiplication Property of Exponents - Answers**
Notes	✓ Exponents are shorthand for repeated multiplication of the same number by itself. For example, instead of 2×2, we can write 2^2. For $3 \times 3 \times 3 \times 3$, we can write 3^4 ✓ In algebra, a variable is a letter used to stand for a number. The most common letters are: $x, y, z, a, b, c, m, and\ n$. ✓ Exponent's rules: $x^a \times x^b = x^{a+b}$, $\dfrac{x^a}{x^b} = x^{a-b}$ $\quad (x^a)^b = x^{a \times b}$ $\qquad (xy)^a = x^a \times y^a$ $\qquad \left(\dfrac{a}{b}\right)^c = \dfrac{a^c}{b^c}$
Example	***Multiply.*** $4x^3 \times 2x^2$ Use Exponent's rules: $x^a \times x^b = x^{a+b} \rightarrow x^3 \times x^2 = x^{3+2} = x^5$ Then: $4x^3 \times 2x^2 = 8x^5$

Your Turn!	1) $x^2 \times 5x = 5x^3$	2) $3x^4 \times x^2 = 3x^6$
	3) $3x^2 \times 4x^5 = 12x^7$	4) $3x^2 \times 6xy = 18x^3y$
	5) $3x^5y \times 5x^2y^3 = 15x^7y^4$	6) $3x^2y^2 \times 5x^2y^8 = 15x^4y^{10}$
	7) $5x^2y \times 5x^2y^7 = 25x^4y^8$	8) $6x^6 \times 4x^9y^4 = 24x^{15}y^4$
Find more at bit.ly/34AWHr1	9) $4x^2y^5 \times 6x^5y^3 = 24x^7y^8$	10) $10x^6x^2 \times 7xy^5 = 70x^9y^5$

Topic	**Division Property of Exponents**
Notes	✓ For division of exponents use these formulas: $\frac{x^a}{x^b} = x^{a-b}$, $x \neq 0$ $\frac{x^a}{x^b} = \frac{1}{x^{b-a}}$, $x \neq 0$, $\qquad \frac{1}{x^b} = x^{-b}$
Example	**Simplify**. $\frac{6x^3y}{36x^2y^3}$ First cancel the common factor: $6 \rightarrow \frac{6x^3y}{36x^2y^3} = \frac{x^3y}{6x^2y^3}$ Use Exponent's rules: $\frac{x^a}{x^b} = x^{a-b} \rightarrow \frac{x^3}{x^2} = x^{3-2} = x^1 = x$ Then: $\frac{6x^3y}{36x^2y^3} = \frac{xy}{6y^3} \rightarrow$ now cancel the common factor: $y \rightarrow \frac{xy}{6y^3} = \frac{x}{6y^2}$
Your Turn! **Find more at** bit.ly/37JAclZ	1) $\frac{2^5}{2^2} =$ 2) $\frac{6x}{12x^3} =$ 3) $\frac{3x^3}{2x^5} =$ 4) $\frac{12x^3}{14x^6} =$ 5) $\frac{12x^3}{9y^8} =$ 6) $\frac{25xy^4}{5x^6y^2} =$ 7) $\frac{2x^4y^5}{7xy^2} =$ 8) $\frac{16x^2y^8}{4x^3} =$ 9) $\frac{9x^4}{12x^7y^9} =$ 10) $\frac{14y^8x^4}{21y^2x^8} =$

Topic	**Division Property of Exponents - Answers**
Notes	✓ For division of exponents use following formulas: $\frac{x^a}{x^b} = x^{a-b}$, $x \neq 0$ $\frac{x^a}{x^b} = \frac{1}{x^{b-a}}$, $x \neq 0$, $\qquad \frac{1}{x^b} = x^{-b}$
Example	**Simplify.** $\frac{6x^3y}{36x^2y^3}$ First cancel the common factor: $6 \rightarrow \frac{6x^3y}{36x^2y^3} = \frac{x^3y}{6x^2y^3}$ Use Exponent's rules: $\frac{x^a}{x^b} = x^{a-b} \rightarrow \frac{x^3}{x^2} = x^{3-2} = x^1 = x$ Then: $\frac{6x^3y}{36x^2y^3} = \frac{xy}{6y^3} \rightarrow$ now cancel the common factor: $y \rightarrow \frac{xy}{6y^3} = \frac{x}{6y^2}$

Your Turn!	1) $\frac{2^5}{2^2} = 2^3$	2) $\frac{6x}{12x^3} = \frac{1}{2x^2}$
	3) $\frac{3x^3}{2x^5} = \frac{3}{2x^2}$	4) $\frac{12x^3}{14x^6} = \frac{6}{7x^3}$
	5) $\frac{12x^3}{9y^8} = \frac{4x^3}{3y^8}$	6) $\frac{25xy^4}{5x^6y^2} = \frac{5y^2}{x^5}$
	7) $\frac{2x^4y^5}{7xy^2} = \frac{2x^3y^3}{7}$	8) $\frac{16x^2y^8}{4x^3} = \frac{4y^8}{x}$
Find more at bit.ly/37JAclZ		
	9) $\frac{9x^4}{12x^7y^9} = \frac{3}{4x^3y^9}$	10) $\frac{14y^8x^4}{21y^2x^8} = \frac{2y^6}{3x^4}$

Topic	**Powers of Products and Quotients**
Notes	✓ For any nonzero numbers a and b and any integer x, $$(ab)^x = a^x \times b^x, \left(\frac{a}{b}\right)^c = \frac{a^c}{b^c}$$
Example	***Simplify.*** $\left(\frac{2x^3}{x}\right)^2$ First cancel the common factor: $x \rightarrow \left(\frac{2x^3}{x}\right)^2 = \left(2x^2\right)^2$ Use Exponent's rules: $(ab)^x = a^x \times b^x$ Then: $\left(2x^2\right)^2 = (2)^2\left(x^2\right)^2 = 4x^4$

Your Turn!	1) $(3x^3 x^3)^3 =$	2) $(2x^3 \times 6x)^2 =$
	3) $(10x^{11}y^3)^2 =$	4) $(9x^7 y^5)^2 =$
	5) $(4x^4 y^6)^3 =$	6) $(3x \times 4y^3)^2 =$
Find more at bit.ly/34CgPJm	7) $\left(\frac{5x}{x^2}\right)^2 =$	8) $\left(\frac{x^4 y^4}{x^2 y^2}\right)^3 =$
	9) $\left(\frac{24x}{4x^6}\right)^2 =$	10) $\left(\frac{x^6}{x^4 y^2}\right)^2 =$

Topic	Powers of Products and Quotients - Answers
Notes	✓ For any nonzero numbers a and b and any integer x, $$(ab)^x = a^x \times b^x, \left(\frac{a}{b}\right)^c = \frac{a^c}{b^c}$$
Example	**Simplify.** $\left(\frac{2x^3}{x}\right)^2$ First cancel the common factor: $x \to \left(\frac{2x^3}{x}\right)^2 = (2x^2)^2$ Use Exponent's rules: $(ab)^x = a^x \times b^x$ Then: $(2x^2)^2 = (2)^2(x^2)^2 = 4x^4$

Your Turn!		
	1) $(3x^3x^3)^3 = 27x^{18}$	2) $(2x^3 \times 6x)^2 = 144x^8$
	3) $(10x^{11}y^3)^2 =$ $100x^{22}y^6$	4) $(9x^7y^5)^2 = 81x^{14}y^{10}$
	5) $(4x^4y^6)^3 = 64\,x^{12}y^{18}$	6) $(3x \times 4y^3)^2 = 144x^2y^6$
Find more at bit.ly/34CgPJm	7) $\left(\frac{5x}{x^2}\right)^2 = \frac{25}{x^2}$	8) $\left(\frac{x^4y^4}{x^2y^2}\right)^3 = x^6y^6$
	9) $\left(\frac{24x}{4x^6}\right)^2 = \frac{36}{x^{10}}$	10) $\left(\frac{x^6}{x^4y^2}\right)^2 = \frac{x^4}{y^4}$

Topic	**Zero and Negative Exponents**
Notes	✓ A negative exponent is the reciprocal of that number with a positive exponent. $(3)^{-2} = \frac{1}{3^2}$ ✓ Zero-Exponent Rule: $a^0 = 1$, this means that anything raised to the zero power is 1. For example: $(28x^2y)^0 = 1$
Example	*Evaluate.* $\left(\frac{1}{3}\right)^{-2} =$ Use negative exponent's rule: $\left(\frac{1}{x^a}\right)^{-2} = (x^a)^2 \rightarrow \left(\frac{1}{3}\right)^{-2} = (3)^2 =$ Then: $(3)^2 = 9$

Your Turn!		
	1) $2^{-4} =$	2) $4^{-3} =$
	3) $7^{-3} =$	4) $1^{-3} =$
	5) $8^{-3} =$	6) $4^{-4} =$
	7) $10^{-3} =$	8) $7^{-4} =$
Find more at bit.ly/3rnkh4	9) $\left(\frac{1}{6}\right)^{-1} =$	10) $\left(\frac{1}{9}\right)^{-2} =$

Topic	Zero and Negative Exponents - Answers
Notes	✓ A negative exponent is the reciprocal of that number with a positive exponent. $(3)^{-2} = \frac{1}{3^2}$ ✓ Zero-Exponent Rule: $a^0 = 1$, this means that anything raised to the zero power is 1. For example: $(28x^2y)^0 = 1$
Example	*Evaluate.* $\left(\frac{1}{3}\right)^{-2} =$ Use negative exponent's rule: $\left(\frac{1}{x^a}\right)^{-2} = (x^a)^2 \rightarrow \left(\frac{1}{3}\right)^{-2} = (3)^2 =$ Then: $(3)^2 = 9$

Your Turn!		
	1) $2^{-4} = \frac{1}{16}$	2) $4^{-3} = \frac{1}{64}$
	3) $7^{-3} = \frac{1}{343}$	4) $1^{-3} = 1$
	5) $8^{-3} = \frac{1}{512}$	6) $4^{-4} = \frac{1}{256}$
Find more at bit.ly/3rnkh4	7) $10^{-3} = \frac{1}{1,000}$	8) $7^{-4} = \frac{1}{2,401}$
	9) $\left(\frac{1}{6}\right)^{-1} = 6$	10) $\left(\frac{1}{9}\right)^{-2} = 81$

Topic	**Negative Exponents and Negative Bases**
Notes	✓ Make the power positive. A negative exponent is the reciprocal of that number with a positive exponent. ✓ The parenthesis is important! 5^{-2} is not the same as $(-5)^{-2}$ $(-5)^{-2} = -\dfrac{1}{5^2}$ and $(-5)^{-2} = +\dfrac{1}{5^2}$
Example	**Simplify.** $\left(-\dfrac{3x}{4yz}\right)^{-3} =$ Use negative exponent's rule: $\left(\dfrac{x^a}{x^b}\right)^{-2} = \left(\dfrac{x^b}{x^a}\right)^2 \rightarrow \left(-\dfrac{3x}{4yz}\right)^{-3} = \left(-\dfrac{4yz}{3x}\right)^3$ Now use exponent's rule: $\left(\dfrac{a}{b}\right)^c = \dfrac{a^c}{b^c} \rightarrow \left(-\dfrac{4yz}{3x}\right)^3 = -\dfrac{4^3 y^3 z^3}{3^3 x^3} = -\dfrac{64y^3 z^3}{27x^3}$
Your Turn!	1) $-4x^{-3}y^{-3} =$ 2) $25x^{-4}y^{-2} =$
	3) $14a^{-6}b^{-7} =$ 4) $-12x^2 y^{-3} =$
	5) $-\dfrac{25}{x^{-6}} =$ 6) $\dfrac{7b}{-9c^{-4}} =$
Find more at bit.ly/3nPROSM	7) $\dfrac{7ab}{a^{-3}b^{-1}} =$ 8) $-\dfrac{5n^{-2}}{10p^{-3}} = -$
	9) $\dfrac{36ab^{-1}}{-3c^{-2}} =$ 10) $\left(\dfrac{5a}{3c}\right)^{-2} =$

Topic	Negative Exponents and Negative Bases - Answers
Notes	✓ Make the power positive. A negative exponent is the reciprocal of that number with a positive exponent. ✓ The parenthesis is important! 5^{-2} is not the same as $(-5)^{-2}$ $$(-5)^{-2} = -\frac{1}{5^2} \text{ and } (-5)^{-2} = +\frac{1}{5^2}$$
Example	*Simplify.* $\left(-\dfrac{3x}{4yz}\right)^{-3} =$ Use negative exponent's rule: $\left(\dfrac{x^a}{x^b}\right)^{-2} = \left(\dfrac{x^b}{x^a}\right)^2 \rightarrow \left(-\dfrac{3x}{4yz}\right)^{-3} = \left(-\dfrac{4yz}{3x}\right)^3$ Now use exponent's rule: $\left(\dfrac{a}{b}\right)^c = \dfrac{a^c}{b^c} \rightarrow \left(-\dfrac{4yz}{3x}\right)^3 = -\dfrac{4^3 y^3 z^3}{3^3 x^3} = -\dfrac{64 y^3 z^3}{27 x^3}$

Your Turn!

Find more at

bit.ly/3nPROSM

1) $-4x^{-3}y^{-3} = -\dfrac{4}{x^3 y^3}$

2) $25x^{-4}y^{-2} = \dfrac{25}{x^4 y^2}$

3) $14a^{-6}b^{-7} = \dfrac{14}{a^6 b^7}$

4) $-12x^2 y^{-3} = -\dfrac{12x^2}{y^3}$

5) $-\dfrac{25}{x^{-6}} = -25x^6$

6) $\dfrac{7b}{-9c^{-4}} = -\dfrac{7bc^4}{9}$

7) $\dfrac{7ab}{a^{-3}b^{-1}} = 7a^4 b^2$

8) $-\dfrac{5n^{-2}}{10p^{-3}} = -\dfrac{p^3}{2n^2}$

9) $\dfrac{36ab^{-1}}{-3c^{-2}} = -\dfrac{12ac^2}{b}$

10) $\left(\dfrac{5a}{3c}\right)^{-2} = \dfrac{9c^2}{25a^2}$

Topic	Scientific Notation
Notes	✓ It is used to write very big or very small numbers in decimal form. ✓ In scientific notation all numbers are written in the form of: $$m \times 10^n$$ | Decimal notation	Scientific notation
3	3×10^0
$-45,000$	-4.5×10^4
0.3	3×10^{-1}
2,122.456	2.122456×10^3	
Example	*Write 0.00054 in scientific notation.* First, move the decimal point to the right so that you have a number that is between 1 and 10. Then: $m = 5.4$ Now, determine how many places the decimal moved in step 1 by the power of 10. Then: $10^{-4} \rightarrow$ When the decimal moved to the right, the exponent is negative. Then: $0.00054 = 5.4 \times 10^{-4}$
Your Turn! **Find more at** bit.ly/3nOwJYP	1) $0.000452 =$ 2) $0.00016 =$ 3) $52,000,000 =$ 4) $21,000 =$ 5) $3 \times 10^{-1} =$ 6) $5 \times 10^{-2} =$ 7) $1.4 \times 10^4 =$ 8) $3 \times 10^{-5} =$

Topic	Scientific Notation – Answers
Notes	✓ It is used to write very big or very small numbers in decimal form. ✓ In scientific notation all numbers are written in the form of: $$m \times 10^n$$ <table><tr><td>**Decimal notation**</td><td>**Scientific notation**</td></tr><tr><td>3</td><td>3×10^0</td></tr><tr><td>$-45,000$</td><td>-4.5×10^4</td></tr><tr><td>0.3</td><td>3×10^{-1}</td></tr><tr><td>2,122.456</td><td>2.122456×10^3</td></tr></table>
Example	**Write 0.00054 in scientific notation.** First, move the decimal point to the right so that you have a number that is between 1 and 10. Then: $m = 5.4$ Now, determine how many places the decimal moved in step 1 by the power of 10. Then: $10^{-4} \rightarrow$ When the decimal moved to the right, the exponent is negative. Then: $0.00054 = 5.4 \times 10^{-4}$
Your Turn! **Find more at** bit.ly/3nOwJYP 	1) $0.000452 = 4.52 \times 10^{-4}$ 2) $0.00016 = 1.6 \times 10^{-4}$ 3) $52,000,000 = 5.2 \times 10^7$ 4) $21,000 = 2.1 \times 10^4$ 5) $3 \times 10^{-1} = 0.3$ 6) $5 \times 10^{-2} = 0.05$ 7) $1.4 \times 10^4 = 14,000$ 8) $3 \times 10^{-5} = 0.00003$

Topic	Radicals
Notes	✓ If n is a positive integer and x is a real number, then: $\sqrt[n]{x} = x^{\frac{1}{n}}$, $\sqrt[n]{xy} = x^{\frac{1}{n}} \times y^{\frac{1}{n}}$, $\sqrt[n]{\frac{x}{y}} = \frac{x^{\frac{1}{n}}}{y^{\frac{1}{n}}}$, and $\sqrt[n]{x} \times \sqrt[n]{y} = \sqrt[n]{xy}$ ✓ A square root of x is a number r whose square is: $r^2 = x$ (r is a square root of x. ✓ To add and subtract radicals, we need to have the same values under the radical. For example: $\sqrt{3} + \sqrt{3} = 2\sqrt{3}$, $3\sqrt{5} - \sqrt{5} = 2\sqrt{5}$
Example	*Evaluate.* $\sqrt{32} + \sqrt{8} =$ **Solution:** Since we do not have the same values under the radical, we cannot add these two radicals. But we can simplify each radical. $\sqrt{32} = \sqrt{16} \times \sqrt{2} = 4\sqrt{2}$ and $\sqrt{8} = \sqrt{4} \times \sqrt{2} = 2\sqrt{2}$ Now, we have the same values under the radical. Then: $$\sqrt{32} + \sqrt{8} = 4\sqrt{2} + 2\sqrt{2} = 6\sqrt{2}$$

Your Turn!	1) $\sqrt{6} \times \sqrt{6} =$	2) $\sqrt{12} \times \sqrt{3} =$
	3) $\sqrt{3} \times \sqrt{27} =$	4) $\sqrt{32} \div \sqrt{2} =$
Find more at bit.ly/2WEATqr	5) $\sqrt{2} + \sqrt{8} =$	6) $\sqrt{27} - \sqrt{3} =$
	7) $3\sqrt{7} - 2\sqrt{7} =$	8) $6\sqrt{5} \times 3\sqrt{5} =$

Topic	Radicals - Answers
Notes	✓ If n is a positive integer and x is a real number, then: $\sqrt[n]{x} = x^{\frac{1}{n}}$, $\sqrt[n]{xy} = x^{\frac{1}{n}} \times y^{\frac{1}{n}}$, $\sqrt[n]{\frac{x}{y}} = \frac{x^{\frac{1}{n}}}{y^{\frac{1}{n}}}$, and $\sqrt[n]{x} \times \sqrt[n]{y} = \sqrt[n]{xy}$ ✓ A square root of x is a number r whose square is: $r^2 = x$ (r is a square root of x. ✓ To add and subtract radicals, we need to have the same values under the radical. For example: $\sqrt{3} + \sqrt{3} = 2\sqrt{3}$, $3\sqrt{5} - \sqrt{5} = 2\sqrt{5}$
Example	***Evaluate.*** $\sqrt{32} + \sqrt{8} =$ **Solution:** Since we do not have the same values under the radical, we cannot add these two radicals. But we can simplify each radical. $\sqrt{32} = \sqrt{16} \times \sqrt{2} = 4\sqrt{2}$ and $\sqrt{8} = \sqrt{4} \times \sqrt{2} = 2\sqrt{2}$ Now, we have the same values under the radical. Then: $$\sqrt{32} + \sqrt{8} = 4\sqrt{2} + 2\sqrt{2} = 6\sqrt{2}$$

Your Turn!		
Find more at bit.ly/2WEATqr	1) $\sqrt{6} \times \sqrt{6} = 6$	2) $\sqrt{12} \times \sqrt{3} = 6$
	3) $\sqrt{3} \times \sqrt{27} = 9$	4) $\sqrt{32} \div \sqrt{2} = 4$
	5) $\sqrt{2} + \sqrt{8} = 3\sqrt{2}$	6) $\sqrt{27} - \sqrt{3} = 2\sqrt{3}$
	7) $3\sqrt{7} - 2\sqrt{7} = \sqrt{7}$	8) $6\sqrt{5} \times 3\sqrt{5} = 90$

Topic	Simplifying Polynomials
Notes	✓ Find "like" terms. (they have same variables with same power). ✓ Use "FOIL". (First–Out–In–Last) for binomials: $$(x + a)(x + b) = x^2 + (b + a)x + ab$$ ✓ Add or Subtract "like" terms using order of operation.
Example	***Simplify this expression.*** $(x + 3)(x - 8) =$ **Solution:** First apply FOIL method: $(a + b)(c + d) = ac + ad + bc + bd$ $(x + 3)(x - 8) = x^2 - 8x + 3x - 24$ Now combine like terms: $x^2 - 8x + 3x - 24 = x^2 - 5x - 24$

Your Turn!		
	1) $-(4x - 3) =$ _____	2) $3(4x + 7) =$ _____
	3) $3x(3x - 4) =$ _____	4) $5x(2x + 8) =$ _____
	5) $-2x(5x + 6) + 5x =$ _____	6) $-4x(8x - 3) - x^2 =$ _____
Find more at bit.ly/3rnAcj8	7) $(x + 4)(x + 5) =$ _____	8) $(x + 2)(x + 8) =$ _____
	9) $-5x^2 + 9x^3 + 10x^2 =$ _____	10) $-6x^5 + 8x^4 + 9x^5 =$ _____

Topic	Simplifying Polynomials – Answers
Notes	✓ Find "like" terms. (they have same variables with same power). ✓ Use "FOIL". (First–Out–In–Last) for binomials: $$(x + a)(x + b) = x^2 + (b + a)x + ab$$ ✓ Add or Subtract "like" terms using order of operation.
Example	***Simplify this expression.*** $(x + 3)(x - 8) =$ **Solution:** First apply FOIL method: $(a + b)(c + d) = ac + ad + bc + bd$ $(x + 3)(x - 8) = x^2 - 8x + 3x - 24$ Now combine like terms: $x^2 - 8x + 3x - 24 = x^2 - 5x - 24$

Your Turn!	1) $-(4x - 3) =$ $-4x + 3$	2) $3(4x + 7) =$ $12x + 21$
	3) $3x(3x - 4) =$ $9x^2 - 12x$	4) $5x(2x + 8) =$ $10x^2 + 40x$
	5) $-2x(5x + 6) + 5x =$ $-10x^2 - 7x$	6) $-4x(8x - 3) - x^2 =$ $-33x^2 + 12x$
Find more at bit.ly/3rnAcj8	7) $(x + 4)(x + 5) =$ $x^2 + 9x + 20$	8) $(x + 2)(x + 8) =$ $x^2 + 10x + 16$
	9) $-5x^2 + 9x^3 + 10x^2 =$ $9x^3 + 5x^2$	10) $-6x^5 + 8x^4 + 9x^5 =$ $3x^5 + 8x^4$

Topic	**Adding and Subtracting Polynomials**
Notes	✓ Adding polynomials is just a matter of combining like terms, with some order of operations considerations thrown in. ✓ Be careful with the minus signs, and don't confuse addition and multiplication!
Example	*Simplify the expressions.* $(3x^2 - 4x^3) - (5x^3 - 8x^2) =$ **Solution:** First use Distributive Property: $-(5x^3 - 8x^2) = -5x^3 + 8x^2$ $\rightarrow (3x^2 - 4x^3) - (5x^3 - 8x^2) = 3x^2 - 4x^3 - 5x^3 + 8x^2$ Now combine like terms: $3x^2 - 4x^3 - 5x^3 + 8x^2 = -9x^3 + 11x^2$

Your Turn!		
	1) $(x^2 - 3x) + (2x^2 - 6) =$ _____	2) $(4x^3 + 2x) - (x^3 + 5) =$ _____
	3) $(x^2 - 5x) + (6x^2 - 5) =$ _____	4) $(8x^2 - 2) - (3x^2 + 7) =$ _____
	5) $(3x^2 + 2) - (2 - 4x^2) =$ _____	6) $(x^3 + x^2) - (x^3 - 10) =$ _____
Find more at bit.ly/2KUqHqQ	7) $(3x^3 - 2x) - (x - x^3) =$ _____	8) $(x - 5x^4) - (2x^4 + 3x) =$ _____
	9) $(8x^3 + 3) - (5 - 4x^3) =$ _____	10) $(9x^2 + 4x^3) - (3x^3 + 2) =$ _____

Topic	Adding and Subtracting Polynomials – Answers
Notes	✓ Adding polynomials is just a matter of combining like terms, with some order of operations considerations thrown in. ✓ Be careful with the minus signs, and don't confuse addition and multiplication!
Example	*Simplify the expressions.* $(3x^2 - 4x^3) - (5x^3 - 8x^2) =$ **Solution:** First use Distributive Property: $-(5x^3 - 8x^2) = -5x^3 + 8x^2$ $\rightarrow (3x^2 - 4x^3) - (5x^3 - 8x^2) = 3x^2 - 4x^3 - 5x^3 + 8x^2$ Now combine like terms: $3x^2 - 4x^3 - 5x^3 + 8x^2 = -9x^3 + 11x^2$

Your Turn!	1) $(x^2 - 3x) + (2x^2 - 6) =$ $3x^2 - 3x - 6$	2) $(4x^3 + 2x) - (x^3 + 5) =$ $3x^3 + 2x - 5$
	3) $(x^2 - 5x) + (6x^2 - 5) =$ $7x^2 - 5x - 5$	4) $(8x^2 - 2) - (3x^2 + 7) =$ $5x^2 - 9$
	5) $(3x^2 + 2) - (2 - 4x^2) =$ $7x^2$	6) $(x^3 + x^2) - (x^3 - 10) =$ $x^2 + 10$
Find more at bit.ly/2KUqHqQ	7) $(3x^3 - 2x) - (x - x^3) =$ $4x^3 - 3x$	8) $(x - 5x^4) - (2x^4 + 3x) =$ $-7x^4 - 2x$
	9) $(8x^3 + 3) - (5 - 4x^3) =$ $12x^3 - 2$	10) $(9x^2 + 4x^3) - (3x^3 + 2) =$ $x^3 + 9x^2 - 2$

Topic	**Multiplying Binomials**
Notes	✓A binomial is a polynomial that is the sum or the difference of two terms, each of which is a monomial. ✓To multiply two binomials, use "FOIL" method. (First–Out–In–Last) $(x + a)(x + b) = x \times x + x \times b + a \times x + a \times b = x^2 + bx + ax + ab$
Example	*Multiply.* $(x - 4)(x + 9) =$ **Solution:** Use "FOIL". (First–Out–In–Last): $(x - 4)(x + 9) = x^2 + 9x - 4x - 36$ Then simplify: $x^2 + 9x - 4x - 36 = x^2 + 5x - 36$

Your Turn!	1) $(x + 4)(x + 4) =$ _____	2) $(x + 4)(x + 3) =$ _____
	3) $(x - 3)(x + 4) =$ _____	4) $(x - 2)(x - 4) =$ _____
	5) $(x + 3)(x + 4) =$ _____	6) $(x + 5)(x + 4) =$ _____
	7) $(x - 6)(x - 5) =$ _____	8) $(x - 5)(x - 5) =$ _____
Find more at bit.ly/3aCsOFL	9) $(x + 3)(x - 5) =$ _____	10) $(x - 6)(x + 4) =$ _____

Topic	Multiplying Binomials – Answers
Notes	✓ A binomial is a polynomial that is the sum or the difference of two terms, each of which is a monomial. ✓ To multiply two binomials, use "FOIL" method. (First–Out–In–Last) $(x + a)(x + b) = x \times x + x \times b + a \times x + a \times b = x^2 + bx + ax + ab$
Example	*Multiply.* $(x - 4)(x + 9) =$ **Solution:** Use "FOIL". (First–Out–In–Last): $(x - 4)(x + 9) = x^2 + 9x - 4x - 36$ Then simplify: $x^2 + 9x - 4x - 36 = x^2 + 5x - 36$

Your Turn!		
Find more at bit.ly/3aCsOFL	1) $(x + 4)(x + 4) =$ $x^2 + 8x + 16$	2) $(x + 4)(x + 3) =$ $x^2 + 7x + 12$
	3) $(x - 3)(x + 4) =$ $x^2 + x - 12$	4) $(x - 2)(x - 4) =$ $x^2 - 6x + 8$
	5) $(x + 3)(x + 4) =$ $x^2 + 7x + 12$	6) $(x + 5)(x + 4) =$ $x^2 + 9x + 20$
	7) $(x - 6)(x - 5) =$ $x^2 - 11x + 30$	8) $(x - 5)(x - 5) =$ $x^2 - 10x + 25$
	9) $(x + 3)(x - 5) =$ $x^2 - 2x - 15$	10) $(x - 6)(x + 4) =$ $x^2 - 2x - 24$

Topic	Multiplying and Dividing Monomials
Notes	✓ When you divide or multiply two monomials you need to divide or multiply their coefficients and then divide or multiply their variables. ✓ In case of exponents with the same base, you need to subtract their powers. ✓ Exponent's rules: $$x^a \times x^b = x^{a+b}, \qquad \frac{x^a}{x^b} = x^{a-b}$$ $$\frac{1}{x^b} = x^{-b}, \quad (x^a)^b = x^{a \times b}$$ $$(xy)^a = x^a \times y^a$$
Example	*Divide expressions.* $\frac{-18x^5y^6}{2xy^2} =$ **Solution:** Use exponents' division rule: $\frac{x^a}{x^b} = x^{a-b}, \frac{x^5}{x} = x^{5-1} = x^4$ and $\frac{y^6}{y^2} = y^4$ Then: $\frac{-18x^5y^6}{2xy^2} = -9x^4y^4$
Your Turn!	1) $(x^6y)(xy^3) =$ ——— 3) $(x^7y^4)(2x^5y^2) =$ ——— 5) $(-6x^8y^7)(4x^6y^9) =$ ——— 7) $\frac{40x^9y^6}{8x^5y^4} =$ ———	2) $(x^5y^2)(x^3y^3) =$ ——— 4) $(3x^5y^4)(4x^6y^3) =$ ——— 6) $(-2x^9y^3)(9x^7y^8) =$ ——— 8) $\frac{-56x^{10}y^{15}}{8x^8y^9} =$ ———

Find more at

bit.ly/2WHp4Q4

Topic	Multiplying and Dividing Monomials - Answers
Notes	✓ When you divide or multiply two monomials you need to divide or multiply their coefficients and then divide or multiply their variables. ✓ In case of exponents with the same base, you need to subtract their powers. ✓ Exponent's rules: $$x^a \times x^b = x^{a+b}, \qquad \frac{x^a}{x^b} = x^{a-b}$$ $$\frac{1}{x^b} = x^{-b}, \quad (x^a)^b = x^{a \times b}$$ $$(xy)^a = x^a \times y^a$$
Example	***Divide expressions.*** $\frac{-18x^5y^6}{2xy^2} =$ **Solution:** Use exponents' division rule: $\frac{x^a}{x^b} = x^{a-b}$, $\frac{x^5}{x} = x^{5-1} = x^4$ and $\frac{y^6}{y^2} = y^4$ Then: $\frac{-18x^5y^6}{2xy^2} = -9x^4y^4$
Your Turn!	1) $(x^6y)(xy^3) =$ x^7y^4 2) $(x^5y^2)(x^3y^3) =$ x^8y^5
	3) $(x^7y^4)(2x^5y^2) =$ $2x^{12}y^6$ 4) $(3x^5y^4)(4x^6y^3) =$ $12x^{11}y^7$
	5) $(-6x^8y^7)(4x^6y^9) =$ $-24x^{14}y^{16}$ 6) $(-2x^9y^3)(9x^7y^8) =$ $-18x^{16}y^{11}$
Find more at bit.ly/2WHp4Q4	7) $\frac{40x^9y^6}{8x^5y^4} =$ $5x^4y^2$ 8) $\frac{-56x^{10}y^{15}}{8x^8y^9} =$ $-7x^2y^6$

Topic	**Multiplying a Polynomial and a Monomial**
Notes	✓ When multiplying monomials, use the product rule for exponents. $x^a \times x^b = x^{a+b}$ ✓ When multiplying a monomial by a polynomial, use the distributive property. $$a \times (b + c) = a \times b + a \times c = ab + ac$$ $$a \times (b - c) = a \times b - a \times c = ab - ac$$
Example	*Multiply expressions.* $4x(5x - 8) =$ **Solution:** Use Distributive Property: $4x(5x - 8) = 4x \times 5x - 4x \times (8) =$ Now, simplify: $4x \times 5x - 4x \times (8) = 20x^2 - 32x$

Your Turn!	1) $4x(3x + y) =$ ____	2) $x(x - 6y) =$ ____
	3) $-x(5x - 3y) =$ ____	4) $4x(x + 5y) =$ ____
	5) $-x(5x + 8y) =$ ____	6) $2x(6x - 7y) =$ ____
Find more at bit.ly/3aBYdx2	7) $-4x(x^3 + 3y^2 - 7x) =$ ____	8) $6x(x^2 - 4y^2 + 3) =$ ____

Topic	Multiplying a Polynomial and a Monomial - Answers
Notes	✓ When multiplying monomials, use the product rule for exponents. $x^a \times x^b = x^{a+b}$ ✓ When multiplying a monomial by a polynomial, use the distributive property. $$a \times (b + c) = a \times b + a \times c = ab + ac$$ $$a \times (b - c) = a \times b - a \times c = ab - ac$$
Example	*Multiply expressions.* $4x(5x - 8) =$ **Solution:** Use Distributive Property: $4x(5x - 8) = 4x \times 5x - 4x \times (8) =$ Now, simplify: $4x \times 5x - 4x \times (8) = 20x^2 - 32x$

Your Turn!

1) $4x(3x + y) =$
$12x^2 + 4xy$

2) $x(x - 6y) =$
$x^2 - 6xy$

3) $-x(5x - 3y) =$
$-5x^2 + 3xy$

4) $4x(x + 5y) =$
$4x^2 + 20xy$

5) $-x(5x + 8y) =$
$-5x^2 - 8xy$

6) $2x(6x - 7y) =$
$12x^2 - 14xy$

Find more at

7) $-4x(x^3 + 3y^2 - 7x) =$
$-4x^4 - 12xy^2 + 28x^2$

8) $6x(x^2 - 4y^2 + 3) =$
$6x^3 - 24xy^2 + 18x$

Topic	**Multiplying Monomials**
Notes	✓ A monomial is a polynomial with just one term: Examples: $5x$ or $7x^2yz^8$. ✓ When you multiply monomials, first multiply the coefficients (a number placed before and multiplying the variable) and then multiply the variables using multiplication property of exponents. $x^a \times x^b = x^{a+b}$
Example	*Multiply.* $(-3xy^4z^5) \times (2x^2y^5z^2) =$ **Solution:** Multiply coefficients and find same variables and use multiplication property of exponents: $x^a \times x^b = x^{a+b}$ $-3 \times 2 = -6$, $x \times x^2 = x^{1+2} = x^3$, $y^4 \times y^5 = y^{4+5} = y^9$, and $z^2 \times z^5 = z^{2+5} = z^7$ Then: $(-3xy^4z^5) \times (2x^2y^5z^2) = -6x^3y^9z^7$

Your Turn!	1) $3x^2 \times 5x^6 =$ _____	2) $6x^7 \times 2x^4 =$ _____
	3) $-2x^2y^4 \times 6x^3y^2 =$ _____	4) $-5x^5y \times 3x^3y^4 =$ _____
Find more at bit.ly/2KLVoP8	5) $8x^7y^5 \times 5x^6y^3 =$ _____	6) $-6x^7y^5 \times (-3x^9y^8) =$ _____
	7) $14x^8y^8z^4 \times 2x^4y^3z =$ _____	8) $-7x^9y^7z^{11} \times 6x^6y^7z^5 =$ _____

Topic	Multiplying Monomials- Answers
Notes	✓ A monomial is a polynomial with just one term: Examples: $5x$ or $7x^2yz^8$. ✓ When you multiply monomials, first multiply the coefficients (a number placed before and multiplying the variable) and then multiply the variables using multiplication property of exponents. $x^a \times x^b = x^{a+b}$
Example	***Multiply.*** $(-3xy^4z^5) \times (2x^2y^5z^2) =$ **Solution:** Multiply coefficients and find same variables and use multiplication property of exponents: $x^a \times x^b = x^{a+b}$ $-3 \times 2 = -6$, $x \times x^2 = x^{1+2} = x^3$, $y^4 \times y^5 = y^{4+5} = y^9$, and $z^2 \times z^5 = z^{2+5} = z^7$ Then: $(-3xy^4z^5) \times (2x^2y^5z^2) = -6x^3y^9z^7$

Your Turn!	1) $3x^2 \times 5x^6 =$
	     $15x^8$
		2) $6x^7 \times 2x^4 =$
		     $12x^{11}$

	3) $-2x^2y^4 \times 6x^3y^2 =$
	     $-12x^5y^6$
		4) $-5x^5y \times 3x^3y^4 =$
		     $-15x^8y^5$

Find more at
 	
bit.ly/2KLVoP8
	5) $8x^7y^5 \times 5x^6y^3 =$
	     $40x^{13}y^8$
		6) $-6x^7y^5 \times (-3x^9y^8) =$
		     $18x^{16}y^{13}$

	7) $14x^8y^8z^4 \times 2x^4y^3z =$ $28x^{12}y^{11}z^5$	8) $-7x^9y^7z^{11} \times 6x^6y^7z^5 =$ $-42x^{15}y^{14}z^{16}$

Topic	Factoring Trinomials
Notes	To factor trinomial, use of the following methods: ✓ "FOIL": $(x + a)(x + b) = x^2 + (b + a)x + ab$ ✓ "Difference of Squares": $$a^2 - b^2 = (a + b)(a - b)$$ $$a^2 + 2ab + b^2 = (a + b)(a + b)$$ $$a^2 - 2ab + b^2 = (a - b)(a - b)$$ ✓ "Reverse FOIL": $x^2 + (b + a)x + ab = (x + a)(x + b)$
Example	**Factor this trinomial.** $x^2 + 12x + 32 =$ **Solution:** Break the expression into groups: $(x^2 + 4x) + (8x + 32)$ Now factor out x from $x^2 + 4x : x(x + 4)$, and factor out 8 from $8x + 32$: $8(x + 4)$ Then: $(x^2 + 4x) + (8x + 32) = x(x + 4) + 8(x + 4)$ Now factor out like term: $(x + 4) \rightarrow (x + 4)(x + 8)$
Your Turn!	1) $x^2 + 3x - 4 =$ ⎯⎯⎯ 2) $x^2 + 4x - 12 =$ ⎯⎯⎯
	3) $x^2 + x - 12 =$ ⎯⎯⎯ 4) $x^2 - 6x + 8 =$ ⎯⎯⎯
Find more at bit.ly/38EpdJA	5) $x^2 + 7x + 12 =$ ⎯⎯⎯ 6) $x^2 + 12x + 32 =$ ⎯⎯⎯
	7) $x^2 + 13x + 30 =$ ⎯⎯⎯ 8) $x^2 - x + 72 =$ ⎯⎯⎯

Topic	Factoring Trinomials – Answers
Notes	To factor trinomial, use of the following methods: ✓ "FOIL": $(x + a)(x + b) = x^2 + (b + a)x + ab$ ✓ "Difference of Squares": $$a^2 - b^2 = (a + b)(a - b)$$ $$a^2 + 2ab + b^2 = (a + b)(a + b)$$ $$a^2 - 2ab + b^2 = (a - b)(a - b)$$ ✓ "Reverse FOIL": $x^2 + (b + a)x + ab = (x + a)(x + b)$
Example	**Factor this trinomial.** $x^2 + 12x + 32 =$ **Solution:** Break the expression into groups: $(x^2 + 4x) + (8x + 32)$ Now factor out x from $x^2 + 4x : x(x + 4)$, and factor out 8 from $8x + 32$: $8(x + 4)$ Then: $(x^2 + 4x) + (8x + 32) = x(x + 4) + 8(x + 4)$ Now factor out like term: $(x + 4) \rightarrow (x + 4)(x + 8)$

Your Turn!	1) $x^2 + 3x - 4 =$ $(x + 4)(x - 1)$	2) $x^2 + 4x - 12 =$ $(x - 2)(x + 6)$
	3) $x^2 + x - 12 =$ $(x - 3)(x + 4)$	4) $x^2 - 6x + 8 =$ $(x - 2)(x - 4)$
Find more at bit.ly/38EpdJA	5) $x^2 + 7x + 12 =$ $(x + 3)(x + 4)$	6) $x^2 + 12x + 32 =$ $(x + 8)(x + 4)$
	7) $x^2 + 13x + 30 =$ $(x + 10)(x + 3)$	8) $x^2 - x - 72 =$ $(x - 9)(x + 8)$

Topic	The Pythagorean Theorem
Notes	✓ In any right triangle: $a^2 + b^2 = c^2$
Example	Right triangle ABC (not shown) has two legs of lengths 18 cm (AB) and 24 cm (AC). What is the length of the third side (BC)? **Solution:** Use Pythagorean Theorem: $a^2 + b^2 = c^2$ Then: $a^2 + b^2 = c^2 \rightarrow 18^2 + 24^2 = c^2 \rightarrow 324 + 576 = c^2$ $c^2 = 900 \rightarrow c = \sqrt{900} = 30\ cm$

Your Turn!

1) _____

8, ?, 6

2) _____

34, 16, ?

3) _____

13, 5, ?

4) _____

10, ?, 8

Topic	The Pythagorean Theorem – Answers
Notes	✓ In any right triangle: $a^2 + b^2 = c^2$
Example	Right triangle ABC (not shown) has two legs of lengths 18 cm (AB) and 24 cm (AC). What is the length of the third side (BC)? **Solution:** Use Pythagorean Theorem: $a^2 + b^2 = c^2$ Then: $a^2 + b^2 = c^2 \rightarrow 18^2 + 24^2 = c^2 \rightarrow 324 + 576 = c^2$ $c^2 = 900 \rightarrow c = \sqrt{900} = 30\ cm$
Your Turn! **Find more at** bit.ly/37Jl08v	1) 10 8, 6, ? 2) 30 16, 34, ? 3) 12 13, 5, ? 4) 6 10, 8, ?

Topic	**Triangles**
Notes	✓ In any triangle the sum of all angles is 180 degrees. ✓ 0Area of a triangle = $\frac{1}{2}$ $(base \times height)$ h b
Example	*What is the area of the following triangle?* 6 16 **Solution:** Use the area formula: Area $= \frac{1}{2}$ $(base \times height)$ $base = 16$ and $height = 6$ Area $= \frac{1}{2}(16 \times 6) = \frac{96}{2} = 48$
Your Turn! **Find more at** bit.ly/3haZrRg	1) _____ 20 12 2) _____ 18 28 3) _____ 20 30 4) _____ 34 40

Topic	Triangles – Answers
Notes	✓ In any triangle the sum of all angles is 180 degrees. ✓ Area of a triangle = $\frac{1}{2}$ ($base \times height$) h b
Example	**What is the area of the following triangle?** 6 16 **Solution:** Use the area formula: Area $= \frac{1}{2}$ ($base \times height$) $base = 16$ and $height = 6$ Area $= \frac{1}{2}(16 \times 6) = \frac{96}{2} = 48$

Your Turn!	1) 120 20 12	2) 252 18 28
Find more at bit.ly/3haZrRg 	3) 300 20 30	4) 680 34 40

Topic	**Polygons**
Notes	Perimeter of a square $= 4 \times side = 4s$ Perimeter of a rectangle $= 2(width + length)$ Perimeter of trapezoid $= a + b + c + d$ Perimeter of a regular hexagon $= 6a$ Perimeter of a parallelogram $= 2(l + w)$
Example	**Find the perimeter of following regular hexagon.** **Solution:** Since the hexagon is regular, all sides are equal. Then: Perimeter of Hexagon $= 6 \times (one\ side)$ Perimeter of Hexagon $= 6 \times (one\ side) = 6 \times 9 = 54\ m$

Your Turn!	5) *(rectangle)* _____ 8 *in* 12 *in*	6) _____ 8 *m* 10 *m* 10 *m* 14 *m*
Find more at bit.ly/3nFNiGi	7) *(regular hexagon)*_____ 5 *m*	8) *(parallelogram)*_____ 9 *in* 11 *in*

Topic	Polygons – Answers
Notes	Perimeter of a square $= 4 \times side = 4s$ Perimeter of a rectangle $= 2(width + length)$ Perimeter of trapezoid $= a + b + c + d$ Perimeter of a regular hexagon $= 6a$ Perimeter of a parallelogram $= 2(l + w)$
Example	***Find the perimeter of following regular hexagon.*** **Solution:** Since the hexagon is regular, all sides are equal. Then: Perimeter of Hexagon $= 6 \times (one\ side)$ Perimeter of Hexagon $= 6 \times (one\ side) = 6 \times 9 = 54\ m$

Your Turn!		
	5) *(rectangle)* 40 in 8 in 12 in	6) 42 m 8 m 10 m 10 m 14 m
Find more at bit.ly/3nFNiGi 	7) *(regular hexagon)* 30 m 5 m	8) *(parallelogram)* 40 in 9 in 11 in

Topic	Circles
Notes	✓ In a circle, variable r is usually used for the radius and d for diameter and π is about 3.14. ✓ $Area\ of\ a\ circle = \pi r^2$ ✓ $Circumference\ of\ a\ circle = 2\pi r$ r
Example	**Find the area of the circle.** **Solution:** Use area formula: $Area = \pi r^2$ $r = 2\ in \rightarrow Area = \pi(2)^2 = 4\pi, \pi = 3.14$ **Then:** $Area = 4 \times 3.14 = 12.56\ in^2$ $2\ in$
Your Turn!	**Find the area of each circle.** ($\pi = 3.14$) 1) _____ 5 cm	2) _____ 10 in **Find the Circumference of each circle.** ($\pi = 3.14$) 3) _____ 8 cm	4) _____ 7 m

Topic	Circles – Answers
Notes	✓ In a circle, variable r is usually used for the radius and d for diameter and π is about 3.14. ✓ *Area of a circle* $= \pi r^2$ ✓ *Circumference of a circle* $= 2\pi r$ r
Example	**Find the area of the circle.** **Solution:** Use area formula: $Area = \pi r^2$ $r = 2\ in \rightarrow Area = \pi(2)^2 = 4\pi, \pi = 3.14$ **Then:** $Area = 4 \times 3.14 = 12.56\ in^2$ $2\ in$

Your Turn!	**Find the area of each circle.** ($\pi = 3.14$)

1) $78.5cm^2$ 5 cm	2) $314\ in^2$ 10 in

Find the Circumference of each circle. ($\pi = 3.14$)

3) $50.24\ cm$ 8 cm	4) $43.96\ m$ 7 m

Find more at

bit.ly/3nJdOP2

Topic	Cubes
Notes	✓ A cube is a three-dimensional solid object bounded by six square sides. ✓ Volume is the measure of the amount of space inside of a solid figure, like a cube, ball, cylinder or pyramid. ✓ Volume of a cube $= (one\ side)^3$ ✓ surface area of cube $= 6 \times (one\ side)^2$
Example	***Find the volume and surface area of the following cube.*** 15 cm **Solution:** Use volume formula: $volume = (one\ side)^3$ Then: $volume = (one\ side)^3 = (15)^3 = 3,375\ cm^3$ Use surface area formula: $surface\ area\ of\ cube: 6(one\ side)^2 = 6(15)^2 = 6(225) = 1,350\ cm^2$
Your Turn!	***Find the volume of each cube.***

1) _____

9 in

2) _____

13 ft

3) _____

14 cm

4) _____

20 m

Topic	Cubes – Answers
Notes	✓ A cube is a three-dimensional solid object bounded by six square sides. ✓ Volume is the measure of the amount of space inside of a solid figure, like a cube, ball, cylinder or pyramid. ✓ Volume of a cube $= (one\ side)^3$ ✓ surface area of cube $= 6 \times (one\ side)^2$
Example	**Find the volume and surface area of the following cube.** 15 cm **Solution:** Use volume formula: $volume = (one\ side)^3$ Then: $volume = (one\ side)^3 = (15)^3 = 3,375\ cm^3$ Use surface area formula: $surface\ area\ of\ cube: 6(one\ side)^2 = 6(15)^2 = 6(225) = 1,350\ cm^2$
Your Turn!	**Find the volume of each cube.**

Find the volume of each cube.

1) $729\ in^3$

        9 *in*

2) $2,197\ ft^3$

        13 *ft*

3) $2,744\ cm^3$

        14 *cm*

4) $8,000\ m^3$

        20 *m*

Find more at

bit.ly/2M6PfOl

Topic	Trapezoids
Notes	✓ A quadrilateral with at least one pair of parallel sides is a trapezoid. ✓ Area of a trapezoid $= \frac{1}{2}h(b_1 + b_2)$
Example	**Calculate the area of the trapezoid.** **Solution:** Use area formula: $A = \frac{1}{2}h(b_1 + b_2)$ $b_1 = 8\ cm$, $b_2 = 12\ cm$ and $h = 14\ cm$ Then: $A = \frac{1}{2}(14)(12 + 8) = 7(20) = 140\ cm^2$
Your Turn!	1) _____ 7 cm 4 cm 10 cm 2) _____ 8 m 10 m 12 m
Find more at bit.ly/3hpKACJ	3) _____ 7 ft 6 ft 15 ft 4) _____ 8 cm 6 cm 12 cm

Topic	Trapezoids – Answers
Notes	✓ A quadrilateral with at least one pair of parallel sides is a trapezoid. ✓ Area of a trapezoid $= \frac{1}{2}h(b_1 + b_2)$ b_2 h b_1

Example	**Calculate the area of the trapezoid.**
	  Solution:
	  Use area formula: $A = \frac{1}{2}h(b_1 + b_2)$
	  $b_1 = 8\ cm$, $b_2 = 12\ cm$ and $h = 14\ cm$
	  Then: $A = \frac{1}{2}(14)(12 + 8) = 7(20) = 140\ cm^2$
	
	$12\ cm$
	$14\ cm$
	$8\ cm$

Your Turn! **Find more at** bit.ly/3hpKACJ	1) $34\ cm^2$ $7\ cm$ $4\ cm$ $10\ cm$ 2) $100\ m^2$ $8\ m$ $10\ m$ $12\ m$ 3) $66\ ft^2$ $7\ ft$ $6\ ft$ $15\ ft$ 4) $60\ cm^2$ $8\ cm$ $6\ cm$ $12\ cm$

Topic	**Rectangular Prisms**
Notes	✓ A solid 3-dimensional object which has six rectangular faces. ✓ Volume of a Rectangular prism $= \boldsymbol{Length \times Width \times Height}$ $Volume = l \times w \times h$ $Surface\ area = 2(wh + lw + lh)$
Example	*Find the volume and surface area of rectangular prism.* **Solution:** Use volume formula: $Volume = l \times w \times h$ Then: $Volume = 4 \times 2 \times 6 = 48\ m^3$ Use surface area formula: $Surface\ area = 2(wh + lw + lh)$ Then: $Surface\ area = 2\big((2 \times 6) + (4 \times 2) + (4 \times 6)\big)$ $\qquad\qquad = 2(12 + 8 + 24) = 2(44) = 88\ m^2$
Your Turn!	*Find the surface area of each Rectangular Prism.*

1) _____

5 ft
10 ft
3 ft

2) _____

8 cm
16 cm
6 cm

3) _____

12 m
18 m
10 m

4) _____

18 in
16 in
12 in

Find more at

bit.ly/3nKm2GT

Topic	Rectangular Prisms - Answers
Notes	✓ A solid 3-dimensional object which has six rectangular faces. ✓ Volume of a Rectangular prism $= \boldsymbol{Length \times Width \times Height}$ $Volume = l \times w \times h$ $Surface\ area = 2(wh + lw + lh)$
Example	**Find the volume and surface area of rectangular prism.** **Solution:** Use volume formula: $Volume = l \times w \times h$ Then: $Volume = 4 \times 2 \times 6 = 48\ m^3$ Use surface area formula: $Surface\ area = 2(wh + lw + lh)$ Then: $Surface\ area = 2\big((2 \times 6) + (4 \times 2) + (4 \times 6)\big)$ $= 2(12 + 8 + 24) = 2(44) = 88\ m^2$
Your Turn!	**Find the surface area of each Rectangular Prism.**

Find the surface area of each Rectangular Prism.

1) $190\ ft^2$

5 ft
10 ft
3 ft

2) $544\ cm^2$

8 cm
16 cm
6 cm

3) $1,032\ m^2$

12 m
18 m
10 m

4) $1,392\ in^2$

18 in
16 in
12 in

Find more at

bit.ly/3nKm2GT

Topic	**Cylinder**
Notes	✓ A cylinder is a solid geometric figure with straight parallel sides and a circular or oval cross section. ✓ *Volume of Cylinder Formula = $\pi(radius)^2 \times height$ $\pi = 3.14$* ✓ *Surface area of a cylinder = $2\pi r^2 + 2\pi rh$*
Example	***Find the volume and Surface area of the follow Cylinder.*** **Solution:** Use volume formula: $Volume = \pi(radius)^2 \times height$ Then: $Volume = \pi(3)^2 \times 12 = 9\pi \times 12 = 108\pi$ $\pi = 3.14$ **then:** $Volume = 108\pi = 339.12\ cm^3$ Use surface area formula: $Surface\ area = 2\pi r^2 + 2\pi rh$ **Then:** $2\pi(3)^2 + 2\pi(3)(12) = 2\pi(9) + 2\pi(36) = 18\pi + 72\pi = 90\pi$ $\pi = 3.14$ **Then:** $Surface\ area = 90 \times 3.14 = 282.6\ cm^2$ *12 cm 3 cm*
Your Turn!	***Find the volume of each Cylinder.*** ($\pi = 3.14$) 1) _____ *8 in 3 in* 2) _____ *14 m 5 m* ***Find the Surface area of each Cylinder.*** ($\pi = 3.14$) 3) _____ *15 ft 9 ft* 4) _____ *12 cm 6 cm*

Find more at

bit.ly/37LtcVM

Topic	**Cylinder – Answers**
Notes	✓ A cylinder is a solid geometric figure with straight parallel sides and a circular or oval cross section. ✓ *Volume of Cylinder Formula* $= \pi(radius)^2 \times height$ $\pi = 3.14$ ✓ *Surface area of a cylinder* $= 2\pi r^2 + 2\pi rh$

Example	**Find the volume and Surface area of the follow Cylinder.** **Solution:** Use volume formula: $Volume = \pi(radius)^2 \times height$ Then: $Volume = \pi(3)^2 \times 12 = 9\pi \times 12 = 108\pi$ $\pi = 3.14$ **then:** $Volume = 108\pi = 339.12\ cm^3$ Use surface area formula: $Surface\ area = 2\pi r^2 + 2\pi rh$ **Then:** $2\pi(3)^2 + 2\pi(3)(12) = 2\pi(9) + 2\pi(36) = 18\pi + 72\pi = 90\pi$ $\pi = 3.14$ **Then:** $Surface\ area = 90 \times 3.14 = 282.6\ cm^2$

Your Turn!

Find the volume of each Cylinder. $(\pi = 3.14)$

1) $226.08\ in^3$

8 in
3 in

2) $1,099\ m^3$

14 m
5 m

Find the Surface area of each Cylinder. $(\pi = 3.14)$

3) $1,356.48\ ft^2$

15 ft
9 ft

4) $678.24\ cm^2$

12 cm
6 cm

Find more at

bit.ly/37LtcVM

Topic	Mean, Median, Mode, and Range of the Given Data
Notes	✓ Mean: $\dfrac{sum\ of\ the\ data}{total\ number\ of\ data\ entires}$ ✓ Mode: value in the list that appears most often. ✓ Median: is the middle number of a group of numbers that have been arranged in order by size. ✓ Range: the difference of largest value and smallest value in the list.
Example	***Find the mode and median of these numbers?*** $16, 10, 6, 3, 1, 16, 2, 4$ **Solution:** Mode: value in the list that appears most often. Number 16 is the value in the list that appears most often (there are two number 16). To find median, write the numbers in order: $1, 2, 3, 4, 6, 10, 16, 16$ Number 4 and 6 are in the middle. Find their average: $\dfrac{4+6}{2} = \dfrac{10}{2} = 5$ The median is 5.

Your Turn!	1) $5, 2, 4, 8, 5, 6$ Mode: _____ Range: _____ Mean: _____ Median: _____	2) $6, 3, 2, 9, 5, 7, 2, 14$ Mode: _____ Range: _____ Mean: _____ Median: _____
Find more at bit.ly/2KO86gg	3) $5, 4, 3, 2, 9, 5, 6, 8, 12$ Mode: _____ Range: _____ Mean: _____ Median: _____	4) $10, 3, 8, 3, 9, 3, 4, 14$ Mode: _____ Range: _____ Mean: _____ Median: _____

Topic	**Mean, Median, Mode, and Range of the Given Data - Answers**
Notes	✓ Mean: $\dfrac{sum\ of\ the\ data}{total\ number\ of\ data\ entires}$ ✓ Mode: value in the list that appears most often. ✓ Median: is the middle number of a group of numbers that have been arranged in order by size. ✓ Range: the difference of largest value and smallest value in the list.
Example	**Find the mode and median of these numbers?** 16, 10, 6, 3, 1, 16, 2, 4 **Solution:** Mode: value in the list that appears most often. Number 16 is the value in the list that appears most often (there are two number 16). To find median, write the numbers in order: 1, 2, 3, 4, 6, 10, 16, 16 Number 4 and 6 are in the middle. Find their average: $\dfrac{4+6}{2} = \dfrac{10}{2} = 5$ The median is 5.

Your Turn!	1) 5, 2, 4, 8, 5, 6	2) 6, 3, 2, 9, 5, 7, 2, 14
	Mode: 5 Range: 6 Mean: 5 Median: 5	Mode: 2 Range: 12 Mean: 6 Median: 5.5
	3) 5, 4, 3, 2, 9, 5, 6, 8, 12	4) 10, 3, 8, 3, 9, 3, 4, 14
Find more at bit.ly/2KO86gg	Mode: 5 Range: 10 Mean: 6 Median: 5	Mode: 3 Range: 11 Mean: 6.75 Median: 6

Topic	Probability Problems
Notes	✓ Probability is the likelihood of something happening in the future. It is expressed as a number between zero (can never happen) to 1 (will always happen). ✓ Probability can be expressed as a fraction, a decimal, or a percent. ✓ Probability formula: $Probability = \dfrac{number\ of\ desired\ outcomes}{number\ of\ total\ outcomes}$
Example	***If there are 3 green balls, 4 red balls, and 10 blue balls in a basket, what is the probability that Jason will pick out a red ball from the basket?*** **Solution:** There are 4 red ball and 17 are total number of balls. Therefore, probability that Jason will pick out a red ball from the basket is 4 out of 17 or $\dfrac{4}{3+4+10} = \dfrac{4}{17}$
Your Turn! **Find more at** bit.ly/3phwk1p	1) A number is chosen at random from 1 to 15. Find the probability of selecting a prime number. (A prime number is a whole number that is only divisible by itself and 1) _____
	2) There are only red and blue cards in a box. The probability of choosing a red card in the box at random is one third. If there are 24 blue cards, how many cards are in the box? _____
	3) A die is rolled, what is the probability that an odd number is obtained? _____

Topic	**Probability Problems – Answers**
Notes	✓ Probability is the likelihood of something happening in the future. It is expressed as a number between zero (can never happen) to 1 (will always happen). ✓ Probability can be expressed as a fraction, a decimal, or a percent. ✓ Probability formula: $Probability = \frac{number\ of\ desired\ outcomes}{number\ of\ total\ outcomes}$
Example	*If there are 3 green balls, 4 red balls, and 10 blue balls in a basket, what is the probability that Jason will pick out a red ball from the basket?* **Solution:** There are 4 red ball and 17 are total number of balls. Therefore, probability that Jason will pick out a red ball from the basket is 4 out of 17 or $\frac{4}{3+4+10} = \frac{4}{17}$
Your Turn!	1) A number is chosen at random from 1 to 15. Find the probability of selecting a prime number. (A prime number is a whole number that is only divisible by itself and 1) $\frac{6}{15} = \frac{2}{5}$ *(There are 6 prime numbers from 1 to 15: 2, 3, 5, 7, 11, 13)*
	2) There are only red and blue cards in a box. The probability of choosing a red card in the box at random is one third. If there are 24 blue cards, how many cards are in the box? 36
Find more at bit.ly/3phwk1p 	3) A die is rolled, what is the probability that an odd number is obtained? $\frac{1}{2}$

Topic	Pie Graph
Notes	✓ A Pie Chart is a circle chart divided into sectors, each sector represents the relative size of each value.
Example	A library has 460 books that include Mathematics, Physics, Chemistry, English and History. Use following graph to answer the question. **What is the number of Physics books?** **Solution:** Number of total books = 460 Percent of Physics books = 25% = 0.25 Then, umber of Physics books: $0.25 \times 460 = 115$ History 10% Mathematics 30% English 15% Chemistry 20% Physics 25%
Your Turn! **Find more at** bit.ly/34ECTDv	The circle graph below shows all Mr. Smith's expenses for last month. Mr. Smith spent $400 for clothes last month. Bills 20% Foods 25% Others 23% Clothes 20% Books 12% Mr. Smith's last month expenses
	1) How much did Mr. Smith spend for his Books last month? _____ 2) How much did Mr. Smith spend for Bills last month? _____ 3) How much did Mr. Smith spend for his foods last month? _____

Topic	Pie Graph
Notes	✓ A Pie Chart is a circle chart divided into sectors, each sector represents the relative size of each value.
Example	A library has 460 books that include Mathematics, Physics, Chemistry, English and History. Use following graph to answer the question. **What is the number of Physics books?** **Solution:** Number of total books $= 460$ Percent of Physics books $= 25\% = 0.25$ Then, umber of Physics books: $$0.25 \times 460 = 115$$
Your Turn! **Find more at** bit.ly/34ECTDv 	The circle graph below shows all Mr. Smith's expenses for last month. Mr. Smith spent \$400 for clothes last month. Mr. Smith's last month expenses
	1) How much did Mr. Smith spend for his Books last month? $240
	2) How much did Mr. Smith spend for Bills last month? $400
	3) How much did Mr. Smith spend for his foods last month? $500

Topic	**Permutations and Combinations**
Notes	✓ Permutations: The number of ways to choose a sample of k elements from a set of n distinct objects where order does matter, and replacements are not allowed. For a permutation problem, use this formula: $$_nP_k = \frac{n!}{(n-k)!}$$ ✓ Combination: The number of ways to choose a sample of r elements from a set of n distinct objects where order does not matter, and replacements are not allowed. For a combination problem, use this formula: $$_nC_r = \frac{n!}{r!\,(n-r)!}$$ ✓ Factorials are products, indicated by an exclamation mark. For example, 4! Equals: $4 \times 3 \times 2 \times 1$. Remember that 0! is defined to be equal to 1.
Example	*How many ways can we pick a team of 4 people from a group of 8?* **Solution:** Since the order doesn't matter, we need to use combination formula where n is 8 and r is 4. Then: $\frac{n!}{r!\,(n-r)!} = \frac{8!}{4!\,(8-4)!} = \frac{8!}{4!\,(4)!} = \frac{8\times7\times6\times5\times4!}{4!\,(4)!} = \frac{8\times7\times6\times5}{4\times3\times2\times1} = \frac{1,680}{24} = 70$
Your Turn!	1) In how many ways can 6 athletes be arranged in a straight line? _____
	2) How many ways can we award a first and second place prize among eight contestants? _____
Find more at bit.ly/34BQgUY	3) In how many ways can we choose 4 players from a team of 10 players? _____

Topic	Permutations and Combinations – Answers
Notes	✓ Permutations: The number of ways to choose a sample of k elements from a set of n distinct objects where order does matter, and replacements are not allowed. For a permutation problem, use this formula: $$_nP_k = \frac{n!}{(n-k)!}$$ ✓ Combination: The number of ways to choose a sample of r elements from a set of n distinct objects where order does not matter, and replacements are not allowed. For a combination problem, use this formula: $$_nC_r = \frac{n!}{r!\,(n-r)!}$$ ✓ Factorials are products, indicated by an exclamation mark. For example, 4! Equals: $4 \times 3 \times 2 \times 1$. Remember that 0! is defined to be equal to 1.
Example	*How many ways can we pick a team of 4 people from a group of 8?* **Solution:** Since the order doesn't matter, we need to use combination formula where n is 8 and r is 4. Then: $\dfrac{n!}{r!\,(n-r)!} = \dfrac{8!}{4!\,(8-4)!} = \dfrac{8!}{4!\,(4)!} = \dfrac{8\times7\times6\times5\times4!}{4!\,(4)!} = \dfrac{8\times7\times6\times5}{4\times3\times2\times1} = \dfrac{1,680}{24} = 70$
Your Turn! **Find more at** bit.ly/34BQgUY 	1) In how many ways can 6 athletes be arranged in a straight line? 720
	2) How many ways can we award a first and second place prize among eight contestants? 56
	3) In how many ways can we choose 4 players from a team of 10 players? 210

Topic	**Function Notation and Evaluation**
Notes	✓ Functions are mathematical operations that assign unique outputs to given inputs. ✓ Function notation is the way a function is written. It is meant to be a precise way of giving information about the function without a rather lengthy written explanation. ✓ The most popular function notation is $f(x)$ which is read "f of x". ✓ To evaluate a function, plug in the input (the given value or expression) for the function's variable (place holder, x).
Example	**Evaluate**: $h(n) = 2n^2 - 2$, find $h(2)$. **Solution:** Substitute n with 2: Then: $h(n) = 2n^2 - 2 \rightarrow h(2) = 2(2)^2 - 2 = 8 - 2 \rightarrow h(2) = 6$
Your Turn! **Find more at** bit.ly/3mls7lF	1) $f(x) = x - 1$, find $f(-2)$ _____ 2) $g(x) = 3x + 2$, find $g(2)$ _____ 3) $g(n) = 2n - 8$, find $g(-1)$ _____ 4) $h(n) = n^2 - 1$, find $h(-2)$ _____ 5) $f(x) = x^2 + 12$, find $f(5)$ _____ 6) $g(x) = 2x^2 - 9$, find $g(-2)$_____ 7) $w(x) = 3x^2 - x$, find $w(2n)$ _____ 8) $p(x) = 2x^3 - 8$, find $p(-2a)$ _____

Topic	**Function Notation and Evaluation – Answers**
Notes	✓ Functions are mathematical operations that assign unique outputs to given inputs. ✓ Function notation is the way a function is written. It is meant to be a precise way of giving information about the function without a rather lengthy written explanation. ✓ The most popular function notation is $f(x)$ which is read "f of x". ✓ To evaluate a function, plug in the input (the given value or expression) for the function's variable (place holder, x).
Example	**Evaluate**: $h(n) = 2n^2 - 2$, find $h(2)$. **Solution:** Substitute n with 2: Then: $h(n) = 2n^2 - 2 \rightarrow h(2) = 2(2)^2 - 2 = 8 - 2 \rightarrow h(2) = 6$

Your Turn!		
	1) $f(x) = x - 1$, find $f(-2)$ $f(-2) = -3$	2) $g(x) = 3x + 2$, find $g(2)$ $g(2) = 8$
	3) $g(n) = 2n - 8$, find $g(-1)$ $g(-1) = -10$	4) $h(n) = n^2 - 1$, find $h(-2)$ $h(-2) = 3$
	5) $f(x) = x^2 + 12$, find $f(5)$ $f(5) = 37$	6) $g(x) = 2x^2 - 9$, find $g(-2)$ $g(-2) = -1$
	7) $w(x) = 3x^2 - x$, find $w(2n)$ $w(3n) = 12n^2 - 2n$	8) $p(x) = 2x^3 - 8$, find $p(-2a)$ $p(-2a) = -16a^3 - 8$

Find more at

bit.ly/3mls7lF

Topic	Adding and Subtracting Functions
Notes	✓ Just like we can add and subtract numbers and expressions, we can add or subtract two functions and simplify or evaluate them. The result is a new function. ✓ For two functions $f(x)$ and $g(x)$, we can create two new functions: $(f+g)(x) = f(x) + g(x)$ and $(f-g)(x) = f(x) - g(x)$
Example	$g(a) = 2a - 5, f(a) = a + 8$, Find: $(g+f)(a)$ **Solution:** $(g+f)(a) = g(a) + f(a)$ Then: $(g+f)(a) = (2a - 5) + (a + 8) = 3a + 3$

Your Turn!		
	1) $g(x) = x - 3$ $h(x) = 2x + 5$ Find: $(h+g)(2)$ _____	2) $f(x) = 2x + 6$ $g(x) = -x - 5$ Find: $(f+g)(3)$ _____
	3) $f(x) = 5x + 8$ $g(x) = 3x - 12$ Find: $(f-g)(-2)$ _____	4) $h(x) = 2x^2 - 10$ $g(x) = 3x + 12$ Find: $(h+g)(3)$ _____
Find more at bit.ly/3hdeFVO	5) $g(x) = 10x - 7$ $h(x) = 3x^2 + 11$ Find: $(h-g)(x)$ _____	6) $h(x) = -x^2 - 15$ $g(x) = 3x^2 + 18$ Find: $(h-g)(a)$ _____

Topic	Adding and Subtracting Functions – Answers
Notes	✓ Just like we can add and subtract numbers and expressions, we can add or subtract two functions and simplify or evaluate them. The result is a new function. ✓ For two functions $f(x)$ and $g(x)$, we can create two new functions: $(f+g)(x) = f(x) + g(x)$ and $(f-g)(x) = f(x) - g(x)$
Example	$g(a) = 2a - 5, f(a) = a + 8,$ **Find:** $(g+f)(a)$ **Solution:** $(g+f)(a) = g(a) + f(a)$ Then: $(g+f)(a) = (2a - 5) + (a + 8) = 3a + 3$

Your Turn!

1) $g(x) = x - 3$

   $h(x) = 2x + 5$
   Find: $(h+g)(2)$

   8

2) $f(x) = 2x + 6$

   $g(x) = -x - 5$
   Find: $(f+g)(3)$

   4

3) $f(x) = 5x + 8$

   $g(x) = 3x - 12$
   Find: $(f-g)(-2)$

   16

4) $h(x) = 2x^2 - 10$

   $g(x) = 3x + 12$
   Find: $(h+g)(3)$

   29

Find more at

bit.ly/3hdeFVO

5) $g(x) = 10x - 7$

   $h(x) = 3x^2 + 11$
   Find: $(h-g)(x)$

   $3x^2 - 10x + 18$

6) $h(x) = -x^2 - 15$

   $g(x) = 3x^2 + 18$
   Find: $(h-g)(a)$

   $-4a^2 - 33$

Topic	**Multiplying and Dividing Functions**
Notes	✓ Just like we can multiply and divide numbers and expressions, we can multiply and divide two functions and simplify or evaluate them. ✓ For two functions $f(x)$ and $g(x)$, we can create two new functions: $$(f.g)(x) = f(x).g(x) \text{ and } \left(\frac{f}{g}\right)(x) = \frac{f(x)}{g(x)}$$
Example	$g(x) = x + 5, f(x) = x - 3$, Find: $(g.f)(2)$ **Solution:** $(g.f)(x) = g(x).f(x) = (x+5)(x-3) = x^2 - 3x + 5x - 15 = x^2 + 2x - 15$ Substitute x with 2: $(g.f)(x) = (2)^2 + 2(2) - 15 = 4 + 4 - 15 = -7$

Your Turn!

1) $g(x) = x - 1$

   $h(x) = x + 2$

   Find: $(g.h)(-3)$

   _____

2) $f(x) = x + 2$

   $g(x) = -x - 3$

   Find: $\left(\frac{f}{g}\right)(-4)$

   _____

3) $f(x) = 5x + 3$

   $g(x) = 2x - 4$

   Find: $\left(\frac{f}{g}\right)(5)$

   _____

4) $h(x) = x^2 - 2$

   $g(x) = x + 4$

   Find: $(g.h)(3)$

   _____

Find more at

bit.ly/3ph7kHA

5) $g(x) = 2x - 8$

   $h(x) = x^2 + 6$

   Find: $(g.h)(-2)$

   _____

6) $h(x) = 3x^2 - 8$

   $g(x) = 4x + 3$

   Find: $\left(\frac{h}{g}\right)(-1)$

   _____

Topic	**Multiplying and Dividing Functions - Answers**
Notes	✓ Just like we can multiply and divide numbers and expressions, we can multiply and divide two functions and simplify or evaluate them. ✓ For two functions $f(x)$ and $g(x)$, we can create two new functions: $(f \cdot g)(x) = f(x) \cdot g(x)$ and $\left(\frac{f}{g}\right)(x) = \frac{f(x)}{g(x)}$
Example	$g(x) = x + 5, f(x) = x - 3$, Find: $(g \cdot f)(2)$ **Solution:** $(g \cdot f)(x) = g(x) \cdot f(x) = (x + 5)(x - 3) = x^2 - 3x + 5x - 15 = x^2 + 2x - 15$ Substitute x with 2: $(g \cdot f)(x) = (2)^2 + 2(2) - 15 = 4 + 4 - 15 = -7$

Your Turn!

1) $g(x) = x - 1$

$h(x) = x + 2$

Find: $(g \cdot h)(-3)$

$(g \cdot h)(-3) = 4$

2) $f(x) = x + 2$

$g(x) = -x - 3$

Find: $\left(\frac{f}{g}\right)(-4)$

$\left(\frac{f}{g}\right)(-4) = -2$

3) $f(x) = 5x + 3$

$g(x) = 2x - 4$

Find: $\left(\frac{f}{g}\right)(5)$

$\left(\frac{f}{g}\right)(5) = \frac{14}{3}$

4) $h(x) = x^2 - 2$

$g(x) = x + 4$

Find: $(g \cdot h)(3)$

$(g \cdot h)(3) = 49$

5) $g(x) = 2x - 8$

$h(x) = x^2 + 6$

Find: $(g \cdot h)(-2)$

$(g \cdot h)(-2) = -120$

6) $h(x) = 3x^2 - 8$

$g(x) = 4x + 3$

Find: $\left(\frac{h}{g}\right)(-1)$

$\left(\frac{h}{g}\right)(-1) = 5$

Find more at

bit.ly/3ph7kHA

Time to test

Time to refine your quantitative reasoning skill with a practice test.

In this section, there are two complete HSPT Mathematics practice tests. Take these tests to simulate the test day experience. After you've finished, score your tests using the answer keys.

Before You Start

- You'll need a pencil, a calculator, and a timer to take the test.

- After you've finished the test, review the answer key to see where you went wrong.

- Use the answer sheet provided to record your answers. (You can cut it out or photocopy it)

- You will receive 1 point for every correct answer. There is no penalty for wrong answers.

Good Luck!

HSPT Mathematics

Practice Test 1

2021-2022

Total number of questions: 64

Total time for two parts: 45 Minutes

Calculators are not allowed for this test.

139

HSPT Practice Tests Answer Sheet

Remove (or photocopy) these answer sheets and use them to complete the practice tests.

HSPT Mathematics Practice Test 1 Answer Sheet		
1 (A) (B) (C) (D)	26 (A) (B) (C) (D)	51 (A) (B) (C) (D)
2 (A) (B) (C) (D)	27 (A) (B) (C) (D)	52 (A) (B) (C) (D)
3 (A) (B) (C) (D)	28 (A) (B) (C) (D)	53 (A) (B) (C) (D)
4 (A) (B) (C) (D)	29 (A) (B) (C) (D)	54 (A) (B) (C) (D)
5 (A) (B) (C) (D)	30 (A) (B) (C) (D)	55 (A) (B) (C) (D)
6 (A) (B) (C) (D)	31 (A) (B) (C) (D)	56 (A) (B) (C) (D)
7 (A) (B) (C) (D)	32 (A) (B) (C) (D)	57 (A) (B) (C) (D)
8 (A) (B) (C) (D)	33 (A) (B) (C) (D)	58 (A) (B) (C) (D)
9 (A) (B) (C) (D)	34 (A) (B) (C) (D)	59 (A) (B) (C) (D)
10 (A) (B) (C) (D)	35 (A) (B) (C) (D)	60 (A) (B) (C) (D)
11 (A) (B) (C) (D)	36 (A) (B) (C) (D)	61 (A) (B) (C) (D)
12 (A) (B) (C) (D)	37 (A) (B) (C) (D)	62 (A) (B) (C) (D)
13 (A) (B) (C) (D)	38 (A) (B) (C) (D)	63 (A) (B) (C) (D)
14 (A) (B) (C) (D)	39 (A) (B) (C) (D)	64 (A) (B) (C) (D)
15 (A) (B) (C) (D)	40 (A) (B) (C) (D)	
16 (A) (B) (C) (D)	41 (A) (B) (C) (D)	
17 (A) (B) (C) (D)	42 (A) (B) (C) (D)	
18 (A) (B) (C) (D)	43 (A) (B) (C) (D)	
19 (A) (B) (C) (D)	44 (A) (B) (C) (D)	
20 (A) (B) (C) (D)	45 (A) (B) (C) (D)	
21 (A) (B) (C) (D)	46 (A) (B) (C) (D)	
22 (A) (B) (C) (D)	47 (A) (B) (C) (D)	
23 (A) (B) (C) (D)	48 (A) (B) (C) (D)	
24 (A) (B) (C) (D)	49 (A) (B) (C) (D)	
25 (A) (B) (C) (D)	50 (A) (B) (C) (D)	

1) If $x = 6$, then $\dfrac{6^6}{x} =$

   A. 30   C. 1,296

   B. 7,776   D. 96

2) Solve for a: $8a - 15 = 9$

   A. 49   C. 32

   B. 0.45   D. 3

3) Sales price of a laptop is $1,912.50, which is 15% off the original price. What is the original price?

   A. $1,952   C. $2,250

   B. $2,000.50   D. $2,460.50

4) $\dfrac{(11\ feet + 7\ yards)}{4} =$ ____

   A. 9 feet   C. 32 feet

   B. 8 feet   D. 4 feet

5) There are only red and blue cards in a box. The probability of choosing a red card in the box at random is one third. If there are 246 blue cards, how many cards are in the box?

   A. 123   C. 328

   B. 308   D. 369

6) Simplify the expression: $(6x^3 - 8x^2 + 2x^4) - (4x^2 - 2x^4 + 2x^3)$

   A. $4x^4 + 4x^3 - 12x^2$ C. $4x^4 + 4x^3 - 12x^2$

   B. $4x^3 - 12x^2$ D. $8x^3 - 12x^2$

7) If Emma can read a page in S minutes, what piece of the page can she read in 20 minutes?

   A. $20S$ C. $20 + S$

   B. $\dfrac{20}{S}$ D. $20 + 2S$

8) If Sam can arrange a storeroom in 2 hours, and Jim can arrange the storeroom in 3 hours, how long will it take for both of them to arrange the storeroom together?

   A. 48 minutes   C. 1 hour and 24 minutes

   B. 1 hour and 12 minutes   D. 1 hour and 36 minutes

9) Jack worked 180 hours this month and made $540. If he works 160 hours next month at the same pay rate, how much will he make?

   A. $480   C. $285

   B. $370   D. $180

10) Which of the following is an irrational number?

   A. $\sqrt{16}$ C. 0.063

   B. $\sqrt{5}$ D. -7

11) What simple interest rate will Ryan need to make $3,000 in interest on a $8,500 principal over 6 years?

   A. 3%   C. 5%

   B. 4%   D. 6%

12) 8 feet, 10 inches + 5 feet, 12 inches = how many inches?

   A. 178 inches   C. 182 inches

   B. 188 inches   D. 200 inches

13) What is the absolute value of -3?

   A. -3 C. 3

   B. 0   D. 5

14) If $(5.2 + 4.3 + 4.5)x = x$, then what is the value of x?

   A. 0   C. 1

   B. $\dfrac{1}{14}$ D. 14

15) While at work, Emma checks her email once every 60 minutes. In 9-hour, how many times does she check her email?

   A. 4 times   C. 9 times

   B. 5 times   D. 6 times

16) Which of the following is a whole number followed by its square?

   A. 2, 8   C. 4, 20

   B. 3, 9   D. 5, 30

17) $8.82 \div 2.4 = \cdots$?

A. 3.675

B. 3.75

C. 3.85

D. 38.52

18) Add $22.07 + 0.035 + 14.3954 + 0.0005 + 20$?

A. 56.42

B. 56.4830

C. 56.5009

D. 56.6203

19) $(12 \div 4) \times (17 - 6)$?

A. 27

B. 29

C. 31

D. 33

20) In the circle seen below, the two lines in the circle are perpendicular. What is the value of x?

A. 6

B. 10

C. 12

D. 14

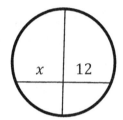

21) The sum of 8 numbers is greater than 160 and less than 240. Which of the following could be the average (arithmetic mean) of the numbers?

A. 20

B. 25

C. 30

D. 35

22) 58% equals:

A. 580

B. 58

C. 5.8

D. 0.58

23) $-20 + 6 \times (-5) - [4 + 22 \times (-4)] \div 2 = ?$

A. -8

B. $\dfrac{3}{4}$

C. -1

D. 8

24) There are 10 more peaches than mangoes in a basket of 48 peaches and mangoes. How many mangoes are in the basket?

A. 31

C. 18

B. 29

D. 15

25) Evaluate $4z + 16$, when $z = -4$

A. -150

C. 50

B. 16

D. 0

26) $12a + 10 = 160$, $a = ?$

A. 12.5

C. 14

B. 10

D. 18.5

27) During a fund-raiser, each of the 35 members of a group sold candy bars. If each member sold an average of five candy bars, how many total bars did the group sell?

A. 35

C. 175

B. 56

D. 225

28) Which of the following is a multiple of 4?

A. 38

C. 85

B. 46

D. 108

29) 10^5 is NOT equal to which of the following?

A. 0.1×10^6

C. $10 \times 10 \times 10 \times 10 \times 10$

B. 10,000

D. $10^2 \times 10^3$

30) What is the improper fraction or mixed number represented by the following figure?

A. $\frac{5}{2}$

B. $\frac{7}{6}$

C. $2\frac{1}{4}$

D. $2\frac{3}{4}$

31) What's the least common multiple (LCM) of 12 and 18?

A. 12 and 18 have no common multiples

C. 112

D. 36

B. 118

32) How many $\frac{1}{6}$ pound paperback books together weigh 30 pounds?

A. 85

C. 105

B. 95

D. 180

33) A woman owns a dog walking business. If 3 workers can walk 6 dogs, how many dogs can 5 workers walk?

A. 10

C. 15

B. 18

D. 25

34) Solve: $0.34 + 0.46$?

A. $\frac{3}{5}$

C. $\frac{2}{3}$

B. $\frac{4}{5}$

D. $\frac{1}{3}$

35) Emily and Daniel have taken the same number of photos on their school trip. Emily has taken 5 times as many as photos as Claire and Daniel has taken 20 more photos than Claire. How many photos has Claire taken?

A. 5

C. 8

B. 6

D. 10

36) The distance between cities A and B is approximately 2,500 miles. If you drive an average of 69 miles per hour, how many hours will it take you to drive from city A to city B?

A. approximately 41 hours

C. approximately 28 hours

B. approximately 36 hours

D. approximately 25 hours

37) If 8 garbage trucks can collect the trash of 40 homes in a day. How many trucks are needed to collect in 150 houses?

A. 15

C. 40

B. 30

D. 45

38) If $x = \frac{4}{7}$ then $\frac{1}{x} = ?$

A. $\frac{7}{4}$

B. $\frac{4}{7}$

C. 4

D. 7

39) Find the square of $\frac{4}{9}$?

A. $\frac{16}{81}$

B. $\frac{81}{16}$

C. $\frac{16}{18}$

D. $\frac{8}{81}$

40) Which of the following is NOT a factor of 50?

A. 5

B. 2

C. 10

D. 15

41) What is the place value of 2 in 4.8325?

A. hundredths

B. thousandths

C. ten thousandths

D. hundred thousandths

42) Which symbol belongs in the circle? 0.542 ◯ 0.0540

A. <

B. >

C. =

D. ≤

43) $(-25) + (-12) =.$

A. 13

B. 10

C. −26

D. −37

44) Use the diagram provided as a reference. If the length between point A and C is 68, and the length between point A and B is 25, what is the length between point B and C?

A. 41

B. 68

C. 31

D. 43

A B C

45) 0.000561 equals:

   A. 5.61×10^4 C. 5.61×10^{-3}

   B. 5.61×10^3 D. 5.61×10^{-4}

46) As a fraction, 0.36 is?

   A. $\frac{3}{36}$ C. $\frac{3}{20}$

   B. $\frac{8}{25}$ D. $\frac{9}{25}$

47) Which of the following is the correct graph for $x \geq 2$ or $x \leq -1$?

   A.

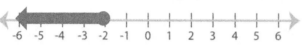

   B.

   C.

   D.

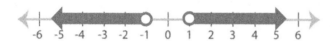

48) Jacob is having a birthday party for his girl and is serving orange juice to the 9 children in attendance. If Jacob has 1 liter of orange juice and wants to divide it equally among the children, how many liters does each child get?

   A. $\frac{1}{8}$ C. $\frac{1}{9}$

   B. $\frac{1}{7}$ D. $\frac{1}{16}$

49) If Frank needs $2\frac{1}{4}$ cup of milk to make a cake. How many cup of milk will he need to make 4 cakes?

   A. 3   C. 9

   B. 6   D. 12

50) If Ella needed to buy 4 bottles of soda for a party in which 10 people attended, how many bottles of soda will she need to buy for a party in which 5 people are attending?

A. 2   C. 10

B. 6   D. 12

51) Which of the following represents the reduced fraction form for 1.9?

A. $2\frac{9}{10}$ C. $\frac{19}{10}$

B. $1\frac{4}{5}$ D. $\frac{36}{20}$

52) If a discount of 20% off the retail price of a chair saves Anna $30. How much did she pay for the chair?

A. $100   C. $120

B. $115   D. $135

53) The fraction $\frac{5}{4}$ can also be written as which of the following?

A. $\frac{4}{3}$ C. 1.25

                                         D. 34.75

B. 0.25

54) Which of the following is equivalent to $7 \times 7 \times 7 \times 7 \times 7$?

A. $\sqrt{7} \times 7$ C. $7 \div 7$

B. 7^5 D. 7,000

55) Emily lives $5\frac{1}{4}$ miles from where she works. When traveling to work, she walks to a bus stop $\frac{1}{3}$ of the way to catch a bus. How many miles away from her house is the bus stop?

A. $4\frac{1}{3}$ miles   C. $2\frac{3}{4}$ miles

B. $4\frac{3}{4}$ miles   D. $1\frac{3}{4}$ miles

56) A bread recipe calls for $2\frac{2}{3}$ cups of flour. If you only have $1\frac{5}{6}$ cups, how much more flour is needed?

A. 1   C. 2

B. $\frac{1}{2}$ D. $\frac{5}{6}$

57) If $l = 3$, $a = 5$ and $b = 3$, then $\frac{4lab}{5} = ?$

   A. 96   C. 48

   B. 24   D. 36

58) Mario loaned Jett $1,300 at a yearly interest rate of 5%. After two year what is the interest owned on this loan?

   A. $130   C. $5

   B. $60   D. $1260

59) In the diagram below, circle A represents the set of all odd numbers, circle B represents the set of all negative numbers, and circle C represents the set of all multiples of 5. Which number could be replaced with y?

   A. 5

   B. 0

   C. −5

   D. −10

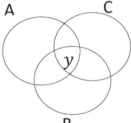

60) Charlotte is 48 years old, twice as old as Avery. How old is Avery?

   A. 24 years old   C. 20 years old

   B. 28 years old   D. 15 years old

61) In the given diagram, the height is 8 cm. what is the area of the triangle?

   A. 28 cm^2

   B. 46 cm^2

   C. 112 cm^2

   D. 252 cm^2

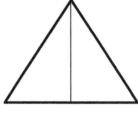

28 cm

62) In the figure below, line A is parallel to line B. What is the value of angle x?

   A. 35 degree

   B. 55 degree

   C. 100 degree

   D. 125 degree

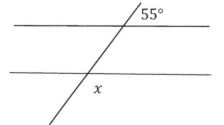

63) Mr. Carlos family are choosing a menu for their reception. They have 3 choices of appetizers, 5 choices of entrees, 4 choices of cake. How many different menu combinations are possible for them to choose?

    A. 12   C. 60

    B. 32   D. 120

64) There are two pizza ovens in a restaurant. Oven 1 burns four times as many pizzas as oven 2. If the restaurant had a total of 15 burnt pizzas on Saturday, how many pizzas did oven 2 burn?

    A. 3   C. 9

    B. 6   D. 12

IF YOU FINISH BEFORE TIME IS CALLED, YOU MAY CHECK YOUR WORK ON THIS SECTION ONLY. DO NOT TURN TO OTHER SECTION IN THE TEST.   **STOP**

HSPT Mathematics

Practice Test 2

2021-2022

Total number of questions: 64

Total time for two parts: 45 Minutes

<u>**Calculators are not allowed for this test.**</u>

HSPT Practice Tests Answer Sheet

Remove (or photocopy) these answer sheets and use them to complete the practice tests.

HSPT Mathematics Practice Test 2 Answer Sheet

#		#		#	
1	Ⓐ Ⓑ Ⓒ Ⓓ	26	Ⓐ Ⓑ Ⓒ Ⓓ	51	Ⓐ Ⓑ Ⓒ Ⓓ
2	Ⓐ Ⓑ Ⓒ Ⓓ	27	Ⓐ Ⓑ Ⓒ Ⓓ	52	Ⓐ Ⓑ Ⓒ Ⓓ
3	Ⓐ Ⓑ Ⓒ Ⓓ	28	Ⓐ Ⓑ Ⓒ Ⓓ	53	Ⓐ Ⓑ Ⓒ Ⓓ
4	Ⓐ Ⓑ Ⓒ Ⓓ	29	Ⓐ Ⓑ Ⓒ Ⓓ	54	Ⓐ Ⓑ Ⓒ Ⓓ
5	Ⓐ Ⓑ Ⓒ Ⓓ	30	Ⓐ Ⓑ Ⓒ Ⓓ	55	Ⓐ Ⓑ Ⓒ Ⓓ
6	Ⓐ Ⓑ Ⓒ Ⓓ	31	Ⓐ Ⓑ Ⓒ Ⓓ	56	Ⓐ Ⓑ Ⓒ Ⓓ
7	Ⓐ Ⓑ Ⓒ Ⓓ	32	Ⓐ Ⓑ Ⓒ Ⓓ	57	Ⓐ Ⓑ Ⓒ Ⓓ
8	Ⓐ Ⓑ Ⓒ Ⓓ	33	Ⓐ Ⓑ Ⓒ Ⓓ	58	Ⓐ Ⓑ Ⓒ Ⓓ
9	Ⓐ Ⓑ Ⓒ Ⓓ	34	Ⓐ Ⓑ Ⓒ Ⓓ	59	Ⓐ Ⓑ Ⓒ Ⓓ
10	Ⓐ Ⓑ Ⓒ Ⓓ	35	Ⓐ Ⓑ Ⓒ Ⓓ	60	Ⓐ Ⓑ Ⓒ Ⓓ
11	Ⓐ Ⓑ Ⓒ Ⓓ	36	Ⓐ Ⓑ Ⓒ Ⓓ	61	Ⓐ Ⓑ Ⓒ Ⓓ
12	Ⓐ Ⓑ Ⓒ Ⓓ	37	Ⓐ Ⓑ Ⓒ Ⓓ	62	Ⓐ Ⓑ Ⓒ Ⓓ
13	Ⓐ Ⓑ Ⓒ Ⓓ	38	Ⓐ Ⓑ Ⓒ Ⓓ	63	Ⓐ Ⓑ Ⓒ Ⓓ
14	Ⓐ Ⓑ Ⓒ Ⓓ	39	Ⓐ Ⓑ Ⓒ Ⓓ	64	Ⓐ Ⓑ Ⓒ Ⓓ
15	Ⓐ Ⓑ Ⓒ Ⓓ	40	Ⓐ Ⓑ Ⓒ Ⓓ		
16	Ⓐ Ⓑ Ⓒ Ⓓ	41	Ⓐ Ⓑ Ⓒ Ⓓ		
17	Ⓐ Ⓑ Ⓒ Ⓓ	42	Ⓐ Ⓑ Ⓒ Ⓓ		
18	Ⓐ Ⓑ Ⓒ Ⓓ	43	Ⓐ Ⓑ Ⓒ Ⓓ		
19	Ⓐ Ⓑ Ⓒ Ⓓ	44	Ⓐ Ⓑ Ⓒ Ⓓ		
20	Ⓐ Ⓑ Ⓒ Ⓓ	45	Ⓐ Ⓑ Ⓒ Ⓓ		
21	Ⓐ Ⓑ Ⓒ Ⓓ	46	Ⓐ Ⓑ Ⓒ Ⓓ		
22	Ⓐ Ⓑ Ⓒ Ⓓ	47	Ⓐ Ⓑ Ⓒ Ⓓ		
23	Ⓐ Ⓑ Ⓒ Ⓓ	48	Ⓐ Ⓑ Ⓒ Ⓓ		
24	Ⓐ Ⓑ Ⓒ Ⓓ	49	Ⓐ Ⓑ Ⓒ Ⓓ		
25	Ⓐ Ⓑ Ⓒ Ⓓ	50	Ⓐ Ⓑ Ⓒ Ⓓ		

1) Raymond wants to invest $5,000 at 4% simple interest rate for 6 years. How much interest will he receive?

A. $1,200

C. $1,500

B. $1,350

D. $1,700

2) If $x = 4$, then $\dfrac{2^3}{x-2} =$

A. 4

C. 2

B. 1

D. 8

3) Over the course of a week, Matt spent $35 on foods. What was the average cost per day?

A. $3.65

C. $4.50

B. $4

D. $5

4) Find $0.00832 \div 2$

A. 0.041

C. 0.0416

B. 0.00416

D. 41.6

5) $-45 + 6 - 12$ equals:

A. 51

C. -53

B. -51

D. 53

6) Multiply 10^6 by 10^3

A. 10^7

C. 10^9

B. 10^8

D. 10^{-9}

7) Find 3.48×10^5

A. 348

C. 34,800

B. 3,480

D. 348,000

8) If a circle has the diameter of 6, what is the area of the circle?

A. 3π

C. 9π

B. 6π

D. 12π

9) What percent of 120 is 45?

   A. 30%

   B. 34.5%

   C. 37.5%

   D. 40%

10) Find the fraction of the grid that is shaded.

   A. $\frac{2}{5}$

   B. $\frac{1}{3}$

   C. $\frac{2}{3}$

   D. $\frac{1}{2}$

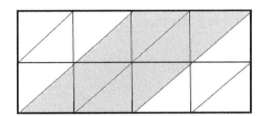

11) If a vehicle is driven 42 miles on Monday, 38 miles on Tuesday, and 34 miles on Wednesday, what is the average number of miles driven each day?

   A. 38 miles

   B. 36 miles

   C. 34 miles

   D. 30 miles

12) In the following right triangle, if the sides AB and AC become twice longer, what will be the ratio of the perimeter of the triangle to its area?

   A. $\frac{1}{2}$

   B. 2

   C. $\frac{1}{3}$

   D. 3

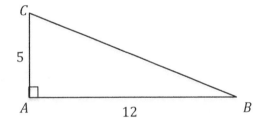

13) Which number sentence is true?

   A. $-10 + 8 > 0$

   B. $|-6 + 7| = 1$

   C. $|-36 - 2| = -38$

   D. $12 + 19 < -2$

14) A student gets an 85% on a test with 40 questions. How many answers did the student solve correctly?

   A. 25

   B. 28

   C. 34

   D. 36

15) 240 Students are in a school. $\frac{3}{5}$ Of these students are boys. How many girls are in the school?

   A. 86   C. 96

   B. 92   D. 108

16) What number is 8 less than $\frac{1}{5}$ of 45?

   A. 0   C. 3

   B. 1   D. 5

17) On a map, 1 cm represents 90 miles. How many miles apart are two cities that are $2\frac{1}{3}$ cm apart on the map?

   A. 150   C. 210

   B. 190   D. 260

18) What is the value of x?

   A. 102

   B. 108

   C. 112

   D. 120

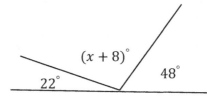

19) What number is $\frac{1}{3}$ of the mean of 5, 3, 14, 22, 12, 6, 1.

   A. 18   C. 5

   B. 10   D. 3

20) $\frac{2}{5}$ of what number is 4 times 3:

   A. 30   C. 18

   B. 26   D. 15

21) $\{2, 5, 7, 16\} \cap \{4, 5, 2, 9\} = ?$

   A. $\{2, 9\}$ C. $\{\ \ \}$

   B. $\{2\}$ D. $\{2, 5\}$

22) What number belongs in the box? $48 + \square = 43$

   A. 5   C. -5

   B. 3   D. 11

23) Simplify: : $1 + 4(-3)^4 =$

   A. -95 C. 325

   B. 186   D. 400

24) Which of the following is a pair of reciprocals?

   A. $(2\frac{1}{5}, \frac{5}{11})$ C. $(1, -1)$

   B. $(5^2, 2^5)$ D. $(-2, 2)$

25) The square root of 180 is between

   A. $13, 14$ C. $15, 16$

   B. $14, 15$ D. $16, 17$

26) $(5 + 7) \div (3^2 \div 3) =$ ___

   A. 12   C. 4

   B. $\frac{5}{7}$ D. 6

27) Solve: $3\frac{3}{8} + 9 =$

   A. $10\frac{1}{8}$ C. $12\frac{3}{7}$

   B. $12\frac{3}{8}$ D. $10\frac{3}{7}$

28) A car is on sale for $18,000, which is a 10% discount off the regular price. What is the regular price?

   A. $20,000   C. $27,000

   B. $23,000   D.$31,000

29) In the following diagram, the straight line is divided by one angled line at 108°. What is the value of a.

A. 66°

B. 90°

C. 72°

D. 180°

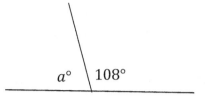

30) 15% of 40 is:

A. 9

B. 6

C. 5

D. 3

31) If $N = 2$ and $\frac{64}{N} + 4 = \square$, then $\square =$ .....

A. 30

B. 32

C. 36

D. 46

32) Emma paid $450 for her bills last month. How much did she pay, on average, per day?

A. $9.30

B. $11

C. $13.50

D. $15

33) If $-7a = 63$, then $a =$ ___

A. -9

B. 9

C. 18

D. 0

34) If $N \times (5 - 3) = 12$ then $N = ?$

A. 6

B. 12

C. 13

D. 14

35) Which of the following is false?

A. $(x + y)z = xz + yz$

B. $x \div y = y(\frac{1}{x})$

C. $(x + y) \div z = \frac{x}{z} + \frac{y}{z}$

D. $x(y + 1) = xy + x$

36) On the number line below, point M is located on line segment ON so that $OM = \frac{1}{3}MN$. What is the position of point M?

A. 1

B. 1.5

C. 2

D. 2.5

$$
\begin{array}{c}
O \qquad\qquad\qquad N \\
\bullet\!\!-\!\!+\!\!-\!\!+\!\!-\!\!+\!\!-\!\!+\!\!-\!\!\bullet\!\!-\!\!+\!\!\rightarrow \\
-6 \quad -4 \quad -2 \quad 0 \quad 2 \quad 4 \quad 6
\end{array}
$$

37) A circus sold 80 student tickets at $1.50 each and 200 adult tickets at $2.00 each. How much was collected?

A. $490

B. $520

C. $550

D. $630

38) Sara has $26 more than three times the amount Emma has. If Sara has $62, how much does Emma has?

A. $12

B. $18.50

C. $26.40

D. $35

39) What are the coordinates of point S on the following graph?

A. $(-2,3)$

B. $(-3,3)$

C. $(-3,4)$

D. $(-1,2)$

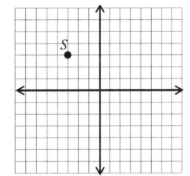

40) Which of the following is equal to 2.5?

A. 3

B. $2\frac{1}{10}$

C. $\frac{25}{10}$

D. $\frac{25}{100}$

41) If 30 is 60% of a number, what is 20% of the same number?

A. 4

B. 6

C. 8

D. 10

42) The number multiplied by 6 is 6 more than 30?

  A. 3   C. 18

  B. 6   D. 36

43) If Steve can paint a room in x hours, what part of the room he can paint in 5 hours?

  A. $\frac{x}{5}$ C. $\frac{5}{x}$

  B. $\frac{1}{5}$ D. $\frac{2}{x}$

44) Which of the following is equal to the expression below? $(2x + y)(x - 2y)$

  A. $4x^2 - 2y^2$ C. $2x^2 - 2y^2 + 2xy$

  B. $2x^2 - 2y^2$ D. $2x^2 - 2y^2 - 3xy$

45) Which answer is equivalent to five to the fifth power?

  A. 0.0005   C. 25

  B. 50,000   D. 3,125

46) The ratio of $\frac{2}{5}$ to $\frac{3}{10}$ is?

  A. 1 to 3   C. 3 to 3

  B. 2 to 3   D. 4 to 3

47) Solve for x: $\left(\frac{5}{4} + \frac{2}{3}\right) - \left(\frac{1}{2} - \frac{1}{3}\right) = x$

  A. $\frac{1}{4}$ C. $2\frac{1}{4}$

  B. $1\frac{3}{4}$ D. $2\frac{3}{4}$

48) $(x + 2)(x + 3) = ?$

  A. $x^2 - 3x + 6$ C. $x^2 + 6x + 5$

  B. $x^2 + 5x + 6$ D. $x^2 + 6x - 5$

49) Examine (X), (Y), and (Z) and find the best answer?
   $(X) = 5^2$, $(Y) = 3 \times 8$, $(Z) = (5 \times 3) + 10$

   A. $(X) = (Y)$ and both are smaller than (Z)

   B. $(X) = (Z)$ and both are greater than (Y)

   C. $(X) + (Y) = (Z)$

   D. $(Y) + (Z) = (X)$

50) $(x^6)^4 = ?$
   A. $2x^6$

   B. x^2

   C. x^{24}

   D. x^{10}

51) $\dfrac{(8\ feet\ +8\ yards)}{4} = \underline{\quad}$
   A. 9 feet

   B. 8 feet

   C. 32 feet

   D. 4 feet

52) Kim spent $35 for pants. This was $10 less than triple what she spent for a shirt. How much was the shirt?
   A. $11

   B. $13

   C. $15

   D. $17

53) $\dfrac{4 \times 9}{5 \times 12} = ?$
   A. $\dfrac{3}{5}$

   B. $\dfrac{3}{4}$

   C. $\dfrac{2}{5}$

   D. $\dfrac{1}{3}$

54) Four hundred thirty-five million eight hundred thousand seven hundred fifteen $= ?$
   A. 435,860,715

   B. 4,247,715

   C. 435,800,715

   D. 43,174,715

55) If $a > 6$, then
   A. $a^2 < 5$

   B. $a^2 > 34$

   C. $a^2 + 6 < 40$

   D. $a^2 - 6 < 28$

56) How many fourths are there in $\frac{5}{8}$?

    A. 4

    B. $2\frac{1}{2}$

    C. $3\frac{1}{8}$

    D. $2\frac{3}{2}$

57) Write 867 in expended form, using exponents.

    A. $(8 \times 10^3) + (6 \times 10^2) + 7$

    B. $(8 \times 10^2) + (6 \times 10) + 7$

    C. $(8 \times 10^3) + (6 \times 10^2) + (7 \times 10)$

    D. $(8 \times 10^3) + (6 \times 10) + 7$

58) The ratio of doctors to nurses in a hospital is $1:3$. If there are 24 doctors in the hospital, how many nurses are there?

    A. 8

    B. 24

    C. 46

    D. 72

59) If $x = 6$, $y = 3$, and $z = 5$, the value of $\sqrt{3y + 2z + x}$ is

    A. 5

    B. $\sqrt{28}$

    C. 9

    D. 15

60) 6 is to 48 as $\frac{3}{8}$ is to?

    A. 3

    B. 6

    C. $\frac{5}{8}$

    D. 8

61) What is the radicand in $\sqrt[3]{216}$?

    A. 3

    B. 72

    C. 36

    D. 6

62) If $x = 7$ what's the value of $6x^2 + 5x - 13$?

    A. 64

    B. 316

    C. 416

    D. 293

63) What is the difference between $(6 \times 10^2) + (2 \times 10)$ and $(7 \times 10^3) + 9$?

    A. 620

    B. 3,326

    C. 6,389

    D. 7,721

64) Find the area of a triangle whose dimensions are $b = 10 \ cm, \ h = 16 \ cm$?

A. $45 \ cm^2$ C. $96 \ cm^2$

B. $80 \ cm^2$ D. $180 \ cm^2$

IF YOU FINISH BEFORE TIME IS CALLED, YOU MAY CHECK YOUR WORK ON THIS SECTION ONLY. DO NOT TURN TO OTHER SECTION IN THE TEST.   **STOP**

HSPT Mathematics Practice Tests Answer Keys

Now, it's time to review your results to see where you went wrong and what areas you need to improve.

HSPT Practice Test 1 Answers

1-	B	17-	A	33-	A	49-	C
2-	D	18-	C	34-	B	50-	A
3-	C	19-	D	35-	A	51-	C
4-	B	20-	C	36-	B	52-	C
5-	D	21-	B	37-	B	53-	C
6-	A	22-	D	38-	A	54-	B
7-	B	23-	A	39-	A	55-	D
8-	B	24-	B	40-	D	56-	D
9-	A	25-	D	41-	B	57-	D
10-	B	26-	A	42-	B	58-	A
11-	C	27-	C	43-	D	59-	C
12-	A	28-	D	44-	D	60-	A
13-	C	29-	B	45-	D	61-	C
14-	A	30-	D	46-	D	62-	D
15-	C	31-	D	47-	C	63-	C
16-	B	32-	D	48-	C	64-	A

HSPT Practice Test 2 Answers

1-	A	17-	C	33-	A	49-	B
2-	A	18-	A	34-	A	50-	C
3-	D	19-	D	35-	B	51-	B
4-	B	20-	A	36-	B	52-	C
5-	B	21-	D	37-	B	53-	A
6-	C	22-	C	38-	A	54-	C
7-	D	23-	C	39-	B	55-	B
8-	C	24-	A	40-	C	56-	B
9-	C	25-	A	41-	D	57-	B
10-	D	26-	C	42-	B	58-	D
11-	A	27-	B	43-	C	59-	A
12-	A	28-	A	44-	D	60-	A
13-	B	29-	C	45-	D	61-	D
14-	C	30-	B	46-	D	62-	B
15-	C	31-	C	47-	B	63-	C
16-	B	32-	D	48-	B	64-	B

HSPT Mathematics Practice Test 1 Explanations

1) Choice B is correct

$\frac{6^6}{6} = 6^5 = 7,776$

2) Choice D is correct

$8a - 15 = 9 \rightarrow 8a = 9 + 15 \rightarrow 8a = 24 \rightarrow a = 3$

3) Choice C is correct

Let x be the original price. Then:

$$\$1,912.50 = x - 0.15(x) \rightarrow 1,912.50 = 0.85x \rightarrow x = \frac{1,912.50}{0.85} \rightarrow x = 2,250.00$$

4) Choice B is correct

$\frac{(11\ feet\ +7\ yards)}{4} = \frac{(11\ feet\ +21\ feet\ )}{4} = \frac{(32\ feet\ )}{4} = 8$ feet

5) Choice D is correct

Let x be total number of cards in the box, then number of red cards is: $x - 246$

The probability of choosing a red card is one third. Then:

Probability $= \frac{1}{3} = \frac{x-246}{x}$

Use cross multiplication to solve for x.

$x \times 1 = 3(x - 246) \rightarrow x = 3x - 738 \rightarrow 2x = 738 \rightarrow x = 369$

6) Choice A is correct

Simplify and combine like terms.

$$(6x^3 - 8x^2 + 2x^4) - (4x^2 - 2x^4 + 2x^3) \rightarrow (6x^3 - 8x^2 + 2x^4) - 4x^2 + 2x^4 - 2x^3$$
$$\rightarrow 4x^4 + 4x^3 - 12x^2$$

7) Choice B is correct

Write a proportion and solve for x: $\frac{1}{S} = \frac{x}{20}$

Solving for variable, x: $Sx = 20 \rightarrow x = \frac{20}{S}$. Emma can read $\frac{20}{S}$ pages, in 20 minutes

8) Choice B is correct

Sam can arrange $\frac{1}{2}$ of the storeroom in 1 hour. Jim can arrange $\frac{1}{3}$ of the storeroom in 1 hour.

When working together, the following equation may be written: $\frac{1}{2}x + \frac{1}{3}x = 1$

Solve for x: $\frac{3x+2x}{6} = 1 \rightarrow \frac{5x}{6} = 1 \rightarrow 5x = 6 \rightarrow x = \frac{6}{5} = 1.2 \rightarrow x = 1$ hour and 12 minutes.

9) Choice A is correct

The following proportion may be used to determine how much Jack will make next month:

$\frac{180}{540} = \frac{160}{x} \rightarrow 180x = 86,400 \rightarrow x = 480$

10) Choice B is correct

$\sqrt{5}$ has a decimal expansion that does not terminate or repeat ($\sqrt{5} = 2.23606789$). Thus, it is an irrational number.

11) Choice D is correct

Simple interest is represented by the formula, $I = Prt$

$3,000 = (8,500)(r)(6) \rightarrow 3,000 = 51,000r \rightarrow r = 0.0588$ or 6%

12) Choice A is correct

1 feet= 12 inches

8 feet, 10 inches $= 106$ inches, 5 feet, 12 inches $= 72$ inches

$106 + 72 = 178$

13) Choice C is correct

The absolute value of a number is the distance the number is from 0. The integer, -3 is 3 units from 0 on the number line. Thus, it has an absolute value of 3.

14) Choice A is correct

$(5.2 + 4.3 + 4.5)x = x$, $14x = x$, Then $x = 0$

15) Choice C is correct

9 hour $= 540$ minutes

$\frac{60}{1} = \frac{540}{x} \rightarrow x = \frac{540}{60} = 9$

16) Choice B is correct

A. $2^2 = 4 \neq 8$

B. $3^2 = 9$

C. $4^2 = 16 \neq 20$

D. $5^2 = 25 \neq 30$

17) Choice A is correct

$8.82 \div 2.4 = 3.675$

18) Choice C is correct

Aligning the decimals at the decimal point and adhering to the same integer addition computation properties, the sum is equal to:

$$22.07 + 0.035 + 14.3954 + 0.0005 + 20 = 56.5009$$

19) Choice D is correct

By first performing the computations within the parentheses, the expression may be rewritten as 3×11, which equals 33.

$$(12 \div 4) \times (17 - 6) = 3 \times 11 = 33$$

20) Choice C is correct

Since the two lines in the circle are perpendicular, then: $x = 12$

21) Choice B is correct

$$160 < 8x < 240 \rightarrow \frac{160}{8} < x < \frac{240}{8} \rightarrow 20 < x < 30 \text{ , then, only choice B, 25, is correct.}$$

22) Choice D is correct

The percentage, 58%, may be converted to a decimal by moving the decimal point two places to left. In other words, 58 is divided by 100, since one percent represents one-hundredth: $58\% = 58 \div 100 = 0.58$

23) Choice A is correct

Use PEMDAS (order of operation):

$$-20 + 6 \times (-5) - [4 + 22 \times (-4)] \div 2 = -20 - 30 - [4 - 88] \div 2 = -50 - [-84] \div 2$$
$$= -50 + 84 \div 2 = -50 + 42 = -8$$

24) Choice B is correct

The problem may be modeled by the following system of equations:

$M = P + 10$ and $M + P = 48$.

Substituting the expression for M, into the second equation, gives:

$$P + 10 + P = 48 \rightarrow 2P = 48 - 10 = 38 \rightarrow P = 19$$

Thus, there are 19 peaches. Since there are 48 peaches and mangoes in all, there must be 29 mangoes.

25) Choice D is correct

$4z + 16 \rightarrow 4(-4) + 16 = 0$

26) Choice A is correct

$12a + 10 = 160 \rightarrow 12a = 160 - 10 \rightarrow 12a = 150 \rightarrow a = 12.5$

27) Choice C is correct

$35 \times 5 = 175$

28) Choice D is correct

A. $\frac{38}{4} = 9.5$, B. $\frac{46}{4} = 11.5$, C. $\frac{85}{4} = 21.25$, D. $\frac{108}{4} = 27$

29) Choice B is correct

$10^5 = 10 \times 10 \times 10 \times 10 \times 10 = 100,000$

30) Choice D is correct

The figure shows 2 completely shaded squares, plus $\frac{3}{4}$. Thus, the figure represents the mixed number, $2\frac{3}{4}$.

31) Choice D is correct

$LCM = 36$

32) Choice D is correct

180 of $\frac{1}{6}$ pound paperback books together weigh 30 pounds.

33) Choice A is correct

Each worker can walk 3 dogs: $6 \div 3 = 2$

5 workers can walk 10 dogs. $5 \times 2 = 10$

34) Choice B is correct

The sum equals 0.80, which may also be written as $\frac{80}{100} = \frac{8}{10} = \frac{4}{5}$

35) Choice A is correct

Emily = Daniel , Emily = 5 Claire

$Daniel = 20 + Claire$

$Emily = Daniel \rightarrow Emily = 20 + Claire$

$Emily = 5\,Claire \rightarrow 5\,Claire = 20 + Claire \rightarrow 5\,Claire\ Claire = 20$

$4\,Claire = 20 \rightarrow Claire = 5$

36) Choice B is correct

$\text{Speed} = \dfrac{distance}{time}$

$69 = \dfrac{2,500}{time} \rightarrow time = \dfrac{2,500}{69} \approx 36.23$

37) Choice B is correct

$\dfrac{8}{40} = \dfrac{x}{150} \rightarrow x = \dfrac{8 \times 150}{40} = 30$

38) Choice A is correct

$\dfrac{1}{x} = \dfrac{\frac{1}{1}}{\frac{4}{7}} = \dfrac{7}{4}$

39) Choice A is correct

The square of the given fraction may be written as $\dfrac{4^2}{9^2}$ or $\dfrac{16}{81}$

40) Choice D is correct

The factors of 50 are: $\{\,1, 2, 5, 10, 25, 50\}$

41) Choice B is correct

2 is in the place value of thousandths in number 4.8325.

42) Choice B is correct

$0.542 > 0.0540$

43) Choice D is correct

The sum of the two negative integers is a negative number.

$(-25) + (-12) = -25 - 12 = -37$

44) Choice D is correct

$68 - 25 = 43$

45) Choice D is correct

Moving the decimal to the right of the 5 gives 5.61×10^{-4}, since the decimal must be moved 4 places to right.

46) Choice D is correct

Digit 3 and 6 end in the hundredths place. This means $0.36 = \frac{36}{100}$. When simplified to simplest form, $\frac{36}{100} = \frac{9}{25}$

47) Choice C is correct

The correct graph should show one ray, with a closed point on the integer -1, which points to the left, and another ray, with a closed point on the integer, 2, which points to the right.

48) Choice C is correct

Divide 1 by 9 children. The answer is $\frac{1}{9}$

49) Choice C is correct

The amount he will need for 4 cakes is equal to the product of $2\frac{1}{4}$ and 4: $2\frac{1}{4} \times 4 = \frac{9}{4} \times 4 = 9$

50) Choice A is correct

$\frac{4}{10} = \frac{x}{5} \rightarrow x = \frac{4 \times 5}{10} = 2$

51) Choice C is correct

$\frac{19}{10} = 1.9$

52) Choice C is correct

The original price of the chair may be found by solving the equation, $0.20x = 30$. Thus, $x = 150$. Since she saves \$30, she pays \$30 less or $\$150 - \$30 = \$120$

53) Choice C is correct

$\frac{5}{4} = 1.25$

54) Choice B is correct

$7 \times 7 \times 7 \times 7 \times 7 = 7^5$

55) Choice D is correct

$\frac{1}{3}$ of the distance is $5\frac{1}{4}$ miles. Then: $\frac{1}{3} \times 5\frac{1}{4} = \frac{1}{3} \times \frac{21}{4} = \frac{21}{12}$

Converting $\frac{21}{12}$ to a mixed number gives: $\frac{21}{12} = 1\frac{9}{12} = 1\frac{3}{4}$

56) Choice D is correct

$$2\frac{2}{3} - 1\frac{5}{6} = 2\frac{4}{6} - 1\frac{5}{6} = \frac{16}{6} - \frac{11}{6} = \frac{5}{6}$$

57) Choice D is correct

$$\frac{4lab}{5} = \frac{4(3)(5)(3)}{5} = 36$$

58) Choice A is correct

Use interest rate formula: $Interest = principal \times rate \times time = 1,300 \times 0.05 \times 2 = 130$

59) Choice C is correct

y is the intersection of the three circles. Therefore, it must be odd (from circle A), negative (from circle B), and multiple of 5 (from circle C).

From the choices, only -5 is odd, negative and multiple of 5.

60) Choice A is correct

Charlotte $= 48$, Charlotte $= 2$ Avery, Avery $= \frac{48}{2} = 24$

61) Choice C is correct

$$A = \frac{1}{2} bh \rightarrow A = \frac{1}{2} (28)(8) = 112$$

62) Choice D is correct

$$180° - 55° = 125° \rightarrow x = 125°$$

63) Choice C is correct

To find the number of possible outfit combinations, multiply number of options for each factor:

$3 \times 5 \times 4 = 60$

64) Choice A is correct

Oven $1 = 4$ oven 2

If Oven 2 burns 3 then oven 1 burns 12 pizzas. $3 + 12 = 15$

HSPT Mathematics Practice Test 2 Explanations

1) Choice A is correct

Simple interest is represented by the formula, $I = prt = (5,000)(0.04)(6) = 1,200$

2) Choice A is correct

$$\frac{2^3}{x-2} = \frac{2^3}{4-2} = \frac{8}{2} = 4$$

3) Choice D is correct

The average is equal to the ratio of the amount spent to the number of days in a week. Thus, the average maybe written as $\frac{35}{7} = 5$. he spent an average of 5 per day.

4) Choice B is correct

$0.00832 \div 2 = 0.00416$

5) Choice B is correct

$-45 + 6 - 12 = -51$

6) Choice C is correct

When multiplying terms with the same base, the exponents should be added. Thus,

$10^6 \times 10^3 = 10^9$

7) Choice D is correct

The decimal will be moved to the right 5 places. Thus 3 zeros will be added to the right of 348, giving $348,000$.

8) Choice C is correct

Diameter $= 6 \rightarrow$ radius $= \frac{6}{2} = 3$

Area of the circle is: πr^2. Substituting 3 for r gives area $= \pi(3)^2 = 9\pi$

9) Choice C is correct

The problem may be modeled as $120x = 45$. Dividing both sides of equation by 120 gives $x = 0.375$ or 37.5%

10) Choice D is correct

There are 16 triangles. Eight of them are shaded. 8 out of 16 is $\frac{8}{16} = \frac{1}{2}$

11) Choice A is correct

Average = $\frac{sum}{total} = \frac{42+38+34}{3} = \frac{114}{3} = 38$

12) Choice A is correct

$AB = 12$ and $AC = 5$. $BC = \sqrt{12^2 + 5^2} = \sqrt{144 + 25} = \sqrt{169} = 13$

Perimeter $= 5 + 12 + 13 = 30$. Area $= \frac{5 \times 12}{2} = 5 \times 6 = 30$

In this case, the ratio of the perimeter of the triangle to its area is: $\frac{30}{30} = 1$

If the sides AB and AC become twice longer, then: $AB = 24$ And $AC = 10$

$BC = \sqrt{24^2 + 10^2} = \sqrt{576 + 100} = \sqrt{676} = 26$. Perimeter $= 26 + 24 + 10 = 60$

Area $= \frac{10 \times 24}{2} = 10 \times 12 = 120$

13) Choice B is correct

$|-6 + 7| = 1 \rightarrow |-1| = 1$

14) Choice C is correct

85% of 40 is: $85\% \ of \ 40 = 0.85 \times 40 = 34$. So, the student solves 34 questions correctly.

15) Choice C is correct

If $\frac{3}{5}$ are boys, so $\frac{2}{5}$ are girls. $\frac{2}{5}$ of 240 equals $\frac{2}{5} \times 240 = 96$

16) Choice B is correct

First find $\frac{1}{5}$ of 45: $\frac{1}{5} \times 45 = 9$. Then subtract: $9 - 8 = 1$

17) Choice C is correct

If $1 \ cm = 90$ miles, then $\frac{1}{3} \ cm = 30$ miles. Therefore, $2\frac{1}{3} \ cm = 2(90) + 30 = 210$

18) Choice A is correct

Sum of the angles of a straight line is 180°.

$48 + 22 + (x + 8) = 180 \rightarrow x + 78 = 180 \rightarrow x = 102$

19) Choice D is correct

Use the mean formula: $\dfrac{some \ of \ the \ values}{number \ of \ values} = \dfrac{5+3+14+22+12+6+1}{7} = \dfrac{63}{7} = 9$

$\dfrac{1}{3}$ of 9 is $\dfrac{1}{3} \times 9 = 3$

20) Choice A is correct

Figure out this problem with algebra: $\dfrac{2}{5}x = 4 \times 3 \rightarrow \dfrac{2}{5}x = 12 \rightarrow x = 12 \times \dfrac{5}{2} = 30$

21) Choice D is correct

The symbol ∩ stands for intersection. The intersection of two or more sets is the set of elements common to both sets. In this case, the common elements are 2 and 5.

22) Choice C is correct

$48 + x = 43 \rightarrow x = 43 - 48 \rightarrow x = -5$

23) Choice C is correct

Start with the operations in the parentheses first: $(-3)^4 = 81$

Then continue with the operations outside the parentheses: $4(-3)^4 = 4(81) = 324$

$1 + 4(-3)^4 = 1 + 324 = 325$

24) Choice A is correct

The reciprocal of a fraction is the fraction reversed. To find the answer, you would have to rename $2\dfrac{1}{5} = \dfrac{11}{5}; \dfrac{11}{5}$ is the reciprocal of $\dfrac{5}{11}$.

25) Choice A is correct

$13^2 = 169$ and $14^2 = 196$. The square root of 180 is between 13 and 14.

26) Choice C is correct

$(5 + 7) \div (3^2 \div 3) = (12) \div (3) = 4$

27) Choice B is correct

First convert mixed number to fraction, then rename the numbers with a common denominator: $\dfrac{27}{8} + 9 = \dfrac{27+72}{8} = \dfrac{99}{8} = 12\dfrac{3}{8}$

28) Choice A is correct

The sale price of the car is 90% of regular price. Thus, the following equation may be used to solve the problem: $18,000 = 0.90x \rightarrow x = 20,000$. Thus, the regular price of the car is $20,000

29) Choice C is correct

$180° - 108° = a° \rightarrow a° = 72°$

30) Choice B is correct

15% of 40: $\frac{15}{100} \times 40 = \frac{15 \times 40}{100} = \frac{600}{100} = 6$

31) Choice C is correct

$N = 2$ and $\frac{64}{N} + 4 = \square$

Then: $\frac{64}{2} + 4 = 32 + 4 = 36$

32) Choice D is correct

There are 30 days in 1 month. If $450 is the total amount paid in a month, the average amount paid per day is $450 \div 30 = $15

33) Choice A is correct

$-7a = 63 \rightarrow a = \frac{63}{-7} = -9$

34) Choice A is correct

$N \times (5 - 3) = 12 \rightarrow N(2) = 12 \rightarrow N = 6$

35) Choice B is correct

Review the choices provided.

A. $(x + y)z = xz + yz$

B. $x \div y = \left(\frac{x}{y}\right) = x\left(\frac{1}{y}\right) \neq y(\frac{1}{x})$

C. $(x + y) \div z = \frac{x}{z} + \frac{y}{z}$

D. $x(y + 1) = xy + x$

36) Choice D is correct

$ON = 4 - (-6) = 10$ units. Let $x = OM$. Then $MN = 10 - x$. Substitute these expressions in the given equation: $x = \frac{1}{3}(10 - x)$. Solve for x:

$$x = \frac{10}{3} - \frac{x}{3} \to x + \frac{x}{3} = \frac{10}{3} \to \frac{4x}{3} = \frac{10}{3} \to 12x = 30 \to x = \frac{30}{12} = 2.5$$

37) Choice B is correct

$80(\$1.50) + 200(\$2.00) = \$520$

38) Choice A is correct

First, subtract $24 from $62: $62 - 26 = 36$

Then, divide by 3: $36 \div 3 = 12$

39) Choice B is correct

The point represents the $x - $ value of -3 and the $y - $ value of 3, thus the ordered pair may be written as $(-3, 3)$

40) Choice C is correct

$\frac{25}{10} = 2.5$

41) Choice D is correct

The first part of the problem may be modeled with the equation, $30 = 0.60x$, solving for x, gives $x = 50$. 20% of 50 may be written as 0.20×50, which equals 10.

42) Choice B is correct

Begin by adding 6 to 30. This number divided by 6 will provide the answer: $30 + 6 = 36 \to 36 \div 6 = 6$

43) Choice C is correct

This is done by ratios. The relationship between part of the room and the whole room is the same as the relationship between the time it takes to paint part of the room and the time it takes to paint the whole room $\to \frac{5}{x}$

44) Choice D is correct

Use FOIL method. $(2x + y)(x - 2y) = 2x^2 - 4xy + xy - 2y^2 = 2x^2 - 3xy - 2y^2$

45) Choice D is correct

Five to the fifth power $= 5^5$, $5^5 = 5 \times 5 \times 5 \times 5 \times 5 = 3{,}125$

46) Choice D is correct

To determine the ratio of the two fractions, multiply them by 10. $\frac{2}{5}$ to $\frac{3}{10} = 4$ to 3

47) Choice B is correct

Rename the fraction with a common denominator. Do the operations in parentheses first.

$$\left(\frac{5}{4}+\frac{2}{3}\right)-\left(\frac{1}{2}-\frac{1}{3}\right)=x \rightarrow \left(\frac{15}{12}+\frac{8}{12}\right)-\left(\frac{3}{6}-\frac{2}{6}\right)=x \rightarrow \frac{23}{12}-\frac{1}{6}=x \rightarrow \frac{23}{12}-\frac{2}{12}=\frac{21}{12}=\frac{7}{4}$$
$$=1\frac{13}{4}$$

48) Choice B is correct

$(x+2)(x+3)=x^2+3x+2x+6=x^2+5x+6$

49) Choice B is correct

$(X)=25$

$(Y)=24$

$(Z)=25$

So $(X)=(Z)$ and both are greater than (Y).

50) Choice C is correct

$(x^6)^4 = x^{6\times4}=x^{24}$

51) Choice B is correct

$\frac{(8\,feet\,+8\,yards)}{4}=\frac{(8\,feet\,+24\,feet\,)}{4}=\frac{(32\,feet\,)}{4}=8$ feet

52) Choice C is correct

Convert everything an equation: $35 = 3 \times$ shirt -10

Now, solve the equation: $45 = 3$ shirt $\rightarrow$ shirt $= \frac{45}{3}=15$

The shirt was $15.

53) Choice A is correct

Multiply and simplify. $\frac{4\times9}{5\times12}=\frac{36}{60}=\frac{3}{5}$

54) Choice C is correct

The millions begin with the seventh digit to the left of the decimal place. Because we need 435 million, we can immediately eliminate choices B and D. Road on: 800 thousand. We need look no further for the correct answer.

55) Choice B is correct

$6^2 = 36$. Because a is greater than 6, a^2 must be greater than 36. Obviously, then, a^2 is greater than 34.

56) Choice B is correct

Divide $\frac{5}{8}$ by $\frac{1}{4}$ to find the answer. $\frac{5}{8} \div \frac{1}{4} = \frac{5}{8} \times \frac{4}{1} = \frac{5}{2} = 2\frac{1}{2}$

57) Choice B is correct

Check each choices:

A. $(8 \times 10^3) + (6 \times 10^2) + 7 = 8,000 + 600 + 7 = 8,607$

B. $(8 \times 10^2) + (6 \times 10) + 7 = 8 + 60 + 3 = 867$

C. $(8 \times 10^3) + (6 \times 10^2) + (7 \times 10) = 8,000 + 600 + 70 = 8,670$

D. $(8 \times 10^3) + (6 \times 10) + 7 = 8,000 + 60 + 7 = 8,067$

Only choice B equal to 867.

58) Choice D is correct

For each doctor, there are 3 nurses. Let x be the number of nurses and set a proportion:
$\frac{1}{3} = \frac{24}{x} \rightarrow x = 72$

59) Choice A is correct

Substitute the values into the expression.

$$\sqrt{3y + 2z + x} = \sqrt{3(3) + 2(5) + 6} = \sqrt{9 + 10 + 6} = \sqrt{25} = 5$$

60) Choice A is correct

6 is one-eighth of 48, and $\frac{3}{8}$ is one-eighth of 3.

61) Choice D is correct

$\sqrt[3]{216} = \sqrt[3]{6^3} = 6$

62) Choice B is correct

Plug in the value of x in the expression. Then: $6x^2 + 5x - 13 = 6(7)^2 + 5(7) - 13 =$

316

63) Choice C is correct

$(6 \times 10^2) + (2 \times 10) = 600 + 20 = 620$

$(7 \times 10^3) + 9 = 7,000 + 9 = 7,009$

The difference is: $7,009 - 620 = 6,389$

64) Choice B is correct

The formula of a triangle is $A = \frac{1}{2}bh = \frac{1}{2} \times 10\ cm \times 16\ cm = 80\ cm^2$

... So Much More Online!

Effortless Math Online HSPT Math Center offers a complete study program, including the following:

✓ Step-by-step instructions on how to prepare for the HSPT Math test

✓ Numerous HSPT Math worksheets to help you measure your math skills

✓ Complete list of HSPT Math formulas

✓ Video lessons for HSPT Math topics

✓ Full-length HSPT Math practice tests

✓ And much more...

No Registration Required.

Receive the PDF version of this book or get another FREE book!

Thank you for using our Book!

Do you LOVE this book?

Then, you can get the PDF version of this book or another book absolutely FREE!

Please email us at:

info@EffortlessMath.com

for details.

Author's Final Note

I hope you enjoyed reading this book. You've made it through the book! Great job!

First of all, thank you for purchasing this study guide. I know you could have picked any number of books to help you prepare for your HSPT Math test, but you picked this book and for that I am extremely grateful.

It took me years to write this study guide for the HSPT Math because I wanted to prepare a comprehensive HSPT Math study guide to help test takers make the most effective use of their valuable time while preparing for the test.

After teaching and tutoring math courses for over a decade, I've gathered my personal notes and lessons to develop this study guide. It is my greatest hope that the lessons in this book could help you prepare for your test successfully.

If you have any questions, please contact me at reza@effortlessmath.com and I will be glad to assist. Your feedback will help me to greatly improve the quality of my books in the future and make this book even better. Furthermore, I expect that I have made a few minor errors somewhere in this study guide. If you think this to be the case, please let me know so I can fix the issue as soon as possible.

If you enjoyed this book and found some benefit in reading this, I'd like to hear from you and hope that you could take a quick minute to post a review on the book's Amazon page. To leave your valuable feedback, please visit: amzn.to/2PLTYGJ

Or scan this QR code.

I personally go over every single review, to make sure my books really are reaching out and helping students and test takers. Please help me help HSPT Math test takers, by leaving a review!

I wish you all the best in your future success!

Reza Nazari

Math teacher and author

Made in the USA
Monee, IL
19 March 2021